DATE DUE

MARY AUSTIN HOLLEY

The Texas Diary, 1835–1838

MARY AUSTIN HOLLEY
The Texas Diary, 1835-1838

EDITED WITH AN INTRODUCTION BY J. P. BRYAN

THE UNIVERSITY OF TEXAS, AUSTIN

published by

THE HUMANITIES RESEARCH CENTER

THE UNIVERSITY OF TEXAS

Distributed by

UNIVERSITY OF TEXAS PRESS

AUSTIN, TEXAS   78712

Printed and bound in the United States of America

Reprint from the TEXAS QUARTERLY

CONTENTS: MARY AUSTIN HOLLEY: *The Texas Diary, 1835–1838*

ABOUT THE CONTRIBUTOR

JAMES PERRY BRYAN is an attorney in Lake Jackson, Texas. A descendant of Stephen F. Austin's sister, Emily Margaret Austin Perry Bryan, he is a member of the Sons of the Republic of Texas and president of the Texas Historical Association. His special interests are Texas history and the collection of old maps, particularly of the southwestern United States and Mexico, some of which have been reproduced in a pamphlet published by the University of Texas. From 1957 to 1963 he was a member of the Board of Regents of The University of Texas.

Portrait of Mary Austin Holley (courtesy of Barker Texas History Center).

MARY AUSTIN HOLLEY : *The Texas Diary, 1835–38*

With Introduction and Notes by J. P. BRYAN

T HE DIARY, REPRODUCED IN ITS ENTIRETY BELOW, COVERS THE PERIOD FROM April 30, 1835, to June 22, 1838. This was only a part of Mary Austin Holley's writings during this period. In addition to her book *Texas,* published in 1836, her letters, poems, newspaper articles, etc., for the period can be found in many of the Mary Austin Holley Collections throughout the United States: University of Texas Archives, Crosby Papers, Aldrich Papers, the Dall Collections, and Collections of Transylvania University.

But who was Mary Austin Holley and what is the importance of this diary? Mrs. Holley may have been one of the best known women in North America during the first part of the nineteenth century, as she certainly was on the western frontier; it is also a fact that she was the first credible historian of Texas, her book *Texas: Observations, Historical, Geographical, and Descriptive, in a Series of Letters Written During a Visit to Austin's Colony with a View to a Permanent Settlement in That County in the Autumn of 1831"* (Baltimore: Armstrong & Plaskitt, 1833), having been the first publication to give an authentic description of that portion of Texas that had been settled by emigrants from North America. The diary—here published for the first time—is important for the realistic picture it gives us of what life was like in one of the first settled areas of Texas—the Coastal Plains near the mouth of the Brazos.

Mary Austin Holley was born in New Haven, Connecticut, in 1784, the fourth child of Elijah Austin and Esther Phelps. The other brothers and sisters were, in the order of age: Horace, Henry, Elijah, Archibald, Henrietta, Jordan Phelps, and Charles. Mary Austin's father was a shipowner and was engaged in what was known as the China Trade. He had had some degree of success prior to his death in 1794 from yellow fever, but when his estate was settled it was found that he had left his family practically destitute. Mary, then ten years old, was reared in the home of her uncle, Timothy Phelps, who was a successful businessman in New Haven. Her surroundings were pleasant, and she received a good education for a woman of that time. She was intelligent, talented, and charming, and evidenced a continuing interest in religion, philosophy, and politics. The few portraits that have been preserved of her indicate that she was an unusually attractive young woman when she married Horace Holley on January 1, 1805.

Horace Holley was one of eight children of Luther Holley and Sarah Dakin, who operated a store in Salisbury, Connecticut. After graduation from Yale, Holley vacillated between law and the ministry, finally deciding on the latter. He was selected by

Hollis Street Church in Boston and spent approximately nine years there. His congregation eventually built a church for him and was eager to have him stay in Boston; the good impression that he made upon his friends and members of the congregation is evidenced by the fact that after his death they raised a trust fund for the education of his minor son. Holley knew intimately such men as John Adams, John Quincy Adams, Henry Clay, Thomas Jefferson, James Monroe, and other leading statesmen, theologians, and writers of his time who held him in high esteem as an intellectual leader.

Evidently both Horace and Mary Holley held liberal theological views, and these views were inclined to disturb conservative leaders and strict theologians, particularly Calvinists. Holley was a convincing speaker and competent teacher, but he did little writing and there is not a great deal of evidence to show the actual merit of his works or effectiveness of his religious theories and philosophy. Also, he could be quite aloof and at times might have been even haughty. As we have noted, he was well established as a minister—certainly a coveted profession at this time in Boston, the cultural center of the East.

A reasonable assumption would be that had he intended to change from the pulpit to the lecture platform he would have sought a position in one of the better eastern institutions. When he was offered the position as head of Transylvania University in the frontier town of Lexington, Kentucky, Mary Holley could see no advantage in the change and used all her influence to keep him from accepting the position, but Horace Holley had made up his mind and Mary went to Lexington resolved to do her best to make the new venture a success.

After nine years, Horace failed in his position as head of Transylvania University. It does not appear that his failure was due to lack of ability as a teacher or administrator but rather because of his liberal theological views and his refusal to compromise with or even recognize the views of his critics, or to assume any political responsibility. When Holley resigned at Transylvania, he had acquired some property and was only forty-six years old. With his background of training and experience (among his accomplishments he had the ability to teach Latin, Greek, Hebrew, Italian, and Spanish), it seems reasonable that he would have returned at this time to the East where his ability would be appreciated and his political views and philosophy tolerated. Instead, he decided to go farther into the frontier and open a boys' school in New Orleans. Although he did have some support from prominent families in the area, whose sons had attended Transylvania during his administration, the school was never opened and it hardly seems probable that a man like Horace Holley could have made a success of such a venture in an area which was so foreign to his background. In 1827, on a trip back to the East, he died of yellow fever, leaving Mary widowed and with little property and two children: a daughter, Harriette, nineteen, who had married William Brand while the family lived in Lexington; and a son, Horace, nine years old and mentally incapacitated.

This lengthy account of Horace Holley, who had been dead several years before the diary was written, is given not only because he was a man of distinction but because as the husband of Mary Austin Holley he had great influence on her throughout her life; it was to perpetuate his accomplishments that she collaborated in the writing of her first book, *A Discourse on the Genius and Character of the Reverend Horace Holley,* published in 1828. After her husband's death, Mary Austin Holley divided her time between the homes of the Labranche family along the German Coast of Louisiana (where she was the tutor for the Labranche children, particularly Melazie Labranche), and that of her daughter in Lexington, or in rented residences in that city. She made five trips to Texas—one involving a stay of over a year—but she had no permanent residence and, as one writer said, she was definitely "on the wing."

Mary Austin Holley's continuing prominence results from her books about Texas and the fact that she was a well-known member of the famous Austin family. Her father was a brother of Moses Austin, who conceived the idea of colonizing Texas and whose plans were carried out by his son Stephen F. Austin. Moses Austin was the first of the Austin clan to follow the trends of the day and go west. He was in the mercantile and lead business, and one of his first stops was in Austinville, Virginia, where his oldest son, Stephen, and his daughter, Emily Margaret, were born. Austin then moved to the Spanish Territory and opened a lead mine named "Mine 'a Burton," which was near the present town of Potosi, Missouri. His early ventures in Missouri were evidently successful, and when Stephen was eleven years old, he sent him East to attend a preparatory school, Bacon Academy in Colchester, Connecticut. It was here that Stephen first met his cousin Mary Austin Holley, who was seven years his senior. Young Stephen Austin also attended Transylvania University for two and a half sessions, but this was prior to the administration of Dr. Holley.

It was through her brother Henry that Mary later became interested in Texas and the activities of her cousin Stephen. She became convinced, after talking with her brother and corresponding with Stephen F. Austin, that something should be written about Texas, and she felt qualified for this undertaking. Also, there is evidence that she felt that she might be able to recoup her fortunes, or rather to make one in Texas.

Her first trip to Texas had been in 1831, when she spent some time at her brother's home at Bolivar on the Brazos, and Stephen F. Austin visited them for several days. There is good reason to believe that a romantic attachment developed between the two rather elderly first cousins. There are probably many circumstances that kept their romance from reaching a culmination; but the information which Mrs. Holley gained at this time from Henry Austin, Stephen F. Austin, and other colonists whom she met along the river, gave her the basic information for the two books she wrote about Texas.

Austin had written her that if she came to Texas and established residence, she would be granted a league of land. She did come, and the land granted her was the tract frequently referred to in her diary as the Dickinson Bayou land. The requirements for establishing a residence in Texas during the time that the area was a part of the Republic of Mexico (Texas and Coahuila) make some very fine legal points. It is doubtful that Mrs. Holley ever set foot on her land.

The present diary begins with Mrs. Holley's second trip to Texas. This was an unrewarding experience from the standpoint both of literary information and financial gain. She was in Texas from April to June, and most of this time was spent again at Bolivar. Boarding at New Orleans, she followed almost exactly the same route as on her first trip. She did little or no writing in her diary except when she was in Texas, so there are only a few entries from July 1835 until December 1837, when she began her third trip to Texas. This time she landed in Galveston, went up Buffalo Bayou to Houston, and then across country to Brazoria, and thence to the mouth of the Brazos, where she took a boat to Galveston, and then back to New Orleans. The trip extended from December 1837 until May 1838.

In reading the diary it is interesting to come upon casual mentions of some of the early leaders of Texas—Stephen F. Austin, Sam Houston, Mirabeau B. Lamar, Samuel May Williams, and Henry Austin. The diary does not develop any unusual historical facts; rather its value lies in the glimpse it gives us of many of the prominent Texans of the colonial period and of the early Republic and in its intimate description of the means of transportation, living conditions, and political and social activities during the infancy of Texas—as well as its description of some of the principal communities then in existence in Texas. Possibly the most interesting aspect of the little hardbacked volume is the fifteen pencil sketches made by Mrs. Holley of the Houston area—showing the capitol building, the Long Row, and home of prominent Houstonians of the time—and of Eagle Island plantation, Phelps plantation, Peach Point, and the warehouse and shipping facilities at the mouth of the Brazos.

The 179-page volume, 6½ x 4″ in size and ¾-inch thick, was written by Mrs. Holley in pencil, but part of it has been retraced by someone using a pen, making it almost illegible in places. Attached unobtrusively inside the front cover is a paper pocket containing newspaper clippings of three of Mrs. Holley's published poems. The diary was evidently given by Mrs. Holley to her daughter Harriette, who in turn gave it to her daughter, Mary Austin Brand Dall, the grandmother of Curtis B. Dall, from whom the University of Texas recently acquired it. The University also acquired a painting of Mary Austin Brand Dall done by Thomas Sully in Baltimore in 1853, which hangs in the Academic Center.

Though this is the first publication of the diary of Mary Austin Holley, it will be evident that we are encountering a writer on whom there is a great deal of information. The life of Mary Austin Holley has been chronicled by two historians: Mattie Austin Hatcher wrote an excellent introduction, "Mary Austin Holley, Her Life and Her Works, 1784–1846," to accompany the republication of Mrs. Holley's letters (Dallas: Southwest Press, 1933); and, more recently, Rebecca Smith Lee has written a comprehensive biography, *Mary Austin Holley* (Austin: University of Texas

MARY AUSTIN HOLLEY

Press, 1962). Also, The Steck Company of Austin in 1935 published a facsimile reproduction of the original 1836 edition of Mrs. Holley's second book, *Texas*. Both of Mrs. Holley's early books on Texas are now collector's items, and recent reports show her *Letters* selling for as much as $500 and *Texas* for $300, something of an increase over the original price of $1.50. Mrs. Holley was an inveterate letter writer, and she carried on an extensive correspondence with her daughter Harriette during all her travels. Most of these letters were preserved, and are still available to scholars.

J. P. BRYAN
Lake Jackson, Texas

1835

April 31st

Schooner San Filipi,[1] 90 tons, Capt. Fuller of Sandwich Massachusetts & his wife[2] —a good yankey lady—like Mrs. Haskell.

Started from the Levée at 6 o'clock evening. Tow boat Livre with 3 other vessels. Arrived at mouth Mississippi 10 o'clock next morning.

May 1st

Started for sea—calm, beautiful weather—scarcely any wind—made little progress for two days. Passengers—60 in number, nearly all seasick.[3] weather though pleasant, hot.

Had to keep my berth all the time except when they spread a blanket for me on deck where all the rest lay—Dr. Hawley, Mr. Treadwell, Mr. Turnbull, Gen. Gaines[4]—many agreeable people on board—such as you meet in steamboats everywhere. Cabin & staterooms arranged as in steamboats—my stateroom was shared with Mrs. *Nibbs*,[5] 3 children & 2 black women—all sick.

May 3rd

Morning a fair breeze sprung up—went on beautifully.

4th

At night, reached mouth of Brazos with great rejoicing.

5th

Morning—all the passengers but Mrs. Pharis & self went ashore amid the breakers in a small lighter. I preferred my chance in the vessel. Red fish, Sheep's head & mullet & crabs for supper & breakfast.

Crossed the bar[6] with difficulty. The Elizabeth after us broke her rudder & stuck fast.

Major Smith[7] and his sister, Mrs. Terry, bound to New Orleans came on board. Heard from my brother's family and wrote letters by them to New Orleans & Lexington.

Touched at McKinney's[8] ware house—a new fabrick since I was here before—on the west side of the river on the point. Surrounded by bales of cotton &c. the appertinance of trade, has a businesslike appearance—a boat was building at this spot, River here 200 yards wide to Brazoria average 150 yds. in some places 300 yds—in others much narrower—water not quite so high as when I was here before—much the same appearance of beauty—a little richer verdure—the livery of spring—hawthorns in blossom thick among the bright green. Birds singing, snakes sunning themselves, sailors killed 4 unsuspecting innocents, guiltless of ruining a world through woman's frailty, at 2 shots. We went on lazily against the current by fits of wind and warping. Had a quiet time—listened to the chattering of the sailors, cook and steward, as by turns I lay in my berth or sat listlessly on the deck—too inert from the recent commotion of my stomach to make further application of my better powers.

I like the honest bluntness of sailors, & the intelligence & knowledge of the world they often display; & can forgive much of the rudeness often unjustly considered criminal.

When tired of talking they would sing—the foreigner his plaintive German or Italian air—our own tars, the familiar church tunes they had learned in their childhood, with the touching associations of father, mother, kindred.

In nature's unawakened solitudes, all sounds speak.

Two return boats, having carried up our passengers yesterday glided by us. A third came along side & called for a rope to board. "Well Charley," exclaimed some of our crew, "how fares it? What do you bring us?" "Only a venison taken last night," answered the *Amphibi*. A fine buck was soon laid on the deck & in speedy preparation for dinner.

May 7th

at noon thermometer, shade, stood at 82°—air so soft & bland from early morning till night, for the luxury & novelty of the thing, there being no gentlemen[9] about, I went without stockings & with the thinnest covering in other respects—the wind always elastic & fresh.

Had radishes to day from Charley, & gathered blackberries on the shore.

Linnarias in flower every where.

We lie to at night & sit late on deck—no dew—air soft & delightful.

A boat heaves in sight descending with more than the oarsmen—a tall gentleman, in broad brim, jumps on our deck. It "is he—it is my brother's voice," I exclaimed. The dusk deceived me. It proved to be Mr. Patton[10] searching for his wife left by us at the mouth.

Among the gossip of Brazoria Mr. Stephenson[11] had killed Mr. Berryman in a duel—muskets at 10 paces. Mr. B. was the lover of Mrs. Stephenson, now parted from her husband in consequence & went to N Orleans last trip of the San Filipi. On the dead body was found a lock of the lady's hair, perforated by the ball that reached his heart—on the envelope was written, as on a bundle of her letters, *"To be placed in my coffin."* Were they so disposed of? No! The injured husband wrote to the faithless wife that the hair she had placed on her lover's bosom, proving no shield, was bathed in his blood.

One of the letters named a place of assignation on the Mississippi, after the husband should have fallen.

The deceitful woman had written back to her husband to kill Berriman for the injury done to her name, or she would never live with him again.

What now will be her position—all destroyed—all lost?

Woman—when bad—how bad!!

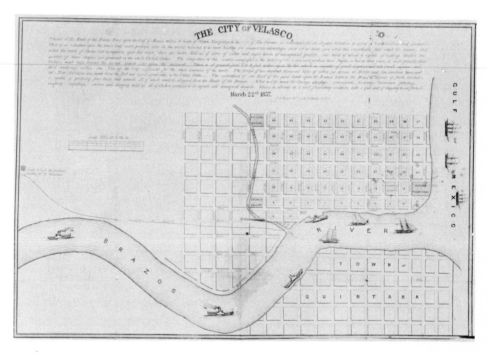

1a. Plat of the City of Velasco, 1837.

3 P.M. 82° on deck, in shade

Still in the Brazos 2 or 3 miles below Brazoria—owing to the prevalence of southerly winds—have to warp nearly all the way. Never was lovelier weather,[12] birds of
every variety of note fill the air with their music. Sometimes they play among our
rigging & perform their various evolutions over our heads.

While at sea a swallow came on board & remained a day or two, no body molesting
it. It was agreeable & seemed a pleasant omen.

This slow way of proceeding makes one realize the full value of steam boats. Never
was a river better calculated for that species of navigation & so is the whole coast
from N Orleans. As we came for instance the sea was smooth as need be required for
a sea steam boat & the coast is indented with safe harbors in case of danger. No doubt
before long steamboats will be used in this trade. One is already on the Brazos & has
been used to tow up vessels. It is at present taking a cargo up to San Felipi or we
might have had the benefit of its assistance. Another just finished at Louisville is
expected every day in N Orleans for the same object.[13]

I forgot to speak in its place of the change that has taken place in Velasco since my
visit in 1831.[14]

Then it was a garrison with a few ragged looking Mexican troops, presenting little
appearance of comfort. Now it has two good boarding houses for the accommodation
of travellers with a domestic look & air of comfort—nothing military in the aspect—
no one to demand passports. On the opposite point, as I mentioned, stands Mc-
Kenny's ware house to increase the show of prosperity.[15]

The bar was much more formidable than when I saw it before—the breakers with
their white caps running high & tumbling with considerable roar. The moment was
interesting as, full of gratitude for our safe passage through the perilous entrance
into our terrestrial paradise. The schooner Elizabeth, which started from N. O. the
night before us & arrived the night before us, in attempting to follow in our wake,
missed the deepest channel & after ineffectual struggles to escape stuck fast & was
much shattered. The crew, ladies & all, escaped by wading to the shore. It is so shal-
low there is never danger of drowning in failure of swimming. I had no use for my
life preserver. This makes the 3d vessel lost here, if she be lost, this season.

Query: might not the drags they use on Lake Erie & other channels thus obstructed
at the mouth be profitably employed here?

Mr. White[16] carried cotton to N. O. brought back $20,000 in goods & $5,000 cash.

About 5 o'clock P.M. our jolly sailors sung their last grand chorus of "cheerily oh,
cheerily oh, cheerily, cheerily oh," at the windlas, as they ushered or rather dragged
us at a snails pace into the famed city of Brazoria. Two well dressed young ladies
stood on the verdant bank listening to our characteristic music as we passed by, and
here & there stood a straggling individual watching our flimsy sails. among those
I recognised the searching eyes of my dear brother—children were paddling about

1. "Velasco, 1835." Velasco was one of the oldest settlements in Stephen F. Austin's colony.

MARY AUSTIN HOLLEY

2. "Entrance to the Brazos—with the bar—a very bad bar. Schooner American aground—Schooner Elizabeth wrecked on Velasco Point."

in the light canoes, otherwise there were none to welcome us, as formerly I had been welcomed in this new land.[17]

There was no rush on board, & on landing there were few persons in the streets. There was an air of desertion that surprised and disappointed me. I expected to find an increase of population & business. On the contrary there was less of each than before. On inquiring into the cause of this unexpected state of things I learned that the new town of Columbia[18] 10 miles above had been made the county town under the new course of things—that there the court was sitting—that—being a new arrangement—all the strangers, with many of the citizens had there fled to witness the proceedings.

Few people stop longer than is necessary at Brazoria, but proceed over the colony to locate their lands.

The cholera,[19] 2 years since, had taken off some families entirely, others in part and new connexions had been formed by the Survivors, (for things proceed rapidly in Texas) & other causes had operated to draw off the population from this once so popular spot. Among these the death, by cholera, of a few enterprising individuals, was probably as great as any. They say there is to be a reaction in other respects. At present there are very good houses without occupants, no inconvenient circumstance for families of new comers who need accommodation *pro tem.* saves exposure by *camping out.*

I can well conceive of disappointment by persons led hither by my description for

I am disappointed myself. But it is not my fault—the thing is changed.

My brother & self lodged at the house of Mrs. E. Andrews[20] where we received much kind attention—& had much talk. Mrs. Andrews has a pretty garden full of growing vegetables—peas in pod & flower. I saw there a fine bed of strawberries propagated from those I brought in 1831, for Mrs. John Austin,[21] now Mrs. Parrot, & moved away. No Austins were left here. Mrs. William Austin[22] & Mr. John Austin formerly so gay and active in all things were missing through cholera, & I felt their loss. Mr. J. A. had fine tracts for a new settlement. Brave, enterprising & generous, he was at the head of all projects for good as well as in parties of mirth. It was he who shared with Col. Austin the first dangers of the colony. It was he who led on to victory at Velasco & Anhuac, but he could not resist super human agency & in an evil hour for the colony—he died—his aged father fell soon after.[23]

3. "McKinney's Warehouse, or Quintana, 1835. Opposite Velasco. Morning." Thomas F. McKinney was a colorful character who figured in early Texas financial history. (See Notes #1 and #8.)

May 10th

Sunday A.M.

With a fair breeze we proceeded on to Belle's Landing,[24] in Marion, the port for the town of Columbia. The river still narrowing & looking diminished, quite unlike my *beau ideal* in some places not more than 150 feet wide our schooner when at right angles as in tacking making a bridge nearly across.

We have been so long ascending I feel very like having encountered an expedition up the Niger or some such river—according to my poor idea of such adventures.

May 11th

Did at length arrive Monday 10 o'clock A.M.

Marion has increased some two or three dwelling houses, & one large ware house built by Mr. White a large dealer in cotton, many bales of which were lying ready to be shipped in our schooner.

They have cut away some of the fine trees here—much to my regret & in some places the banks have caved in, which together with the increased traffic, business demonstrations & the low stage of the river, have destroyed much of the picturesque effects I admired on my former visit.

3 families, passengers in the Elizabeth, landed from a perogue, soon after us. 2 from Alabama, 1 from Baltimore, with a number of negroes.

Back from Marion about 2 miles is the town of Columbia the seat of justice for [? the county] contains a new hotel kept by Bell[25]—new & spacious, the largest building there. There is besides a building or two for Court house offices, &c. This town is on the edge of the prairie, & the scenery is pretty about it. A broad road through timber is cut to the landing—very muddy in wet weather. It is thought by many that this place will not be found so convenient for the Court as Brazoria and that it will before long be removed thither. It is more central but has less accommodation and is too far from the river—so important for transportation.

My brother, Mr. Henry Austin,[26] was in waiting for me at the landing with two horses. After dinner, having arranged for the transporting of my baggage &c. by water to Bolivar,[27] 10 miles, for the moderate price of $12—I mounted and we proceeded to Columbia, I found at the hotel several of my fellow passengers—enjoying the luxury of comfortable repose. Others had proceeded in various directions. After a little chat in which they expressed themselves well pleased with their position and prospects, we proceeded over the prairie to the residence of Dr. Phelps,[28] 12 miles—the longest it seemed to me I ever traveled. It was, however, charming scenery, especially when the sun was sinking. We could generally see the horizon in all directions. Some times the path led through a point of timber land or through a fine grove. At one time 3 deer crossed the road at a few rods before us at the top of their speed and were soon lost in the distance, exciting no remark, so usual is the circumstance. Two gentlemen joined us in our ride enlivening us by their conversation.

We arrived at last at 7 o'clock in the evening & so tired was I that I could scarcely stand or walk. 15 miles on horseback, after 12 days of inaction in the vessel proved a little severe. A cup of good coffee, a refreshing bath, & a good night's rest, however, restored me to comfortable feeling. I can hardly express the sense of luxury I experienced in a bed large enough to stretch myself upon it, with a good mosquito bar which I realized this night.

I awoke with fresh spirits & a good appetite, increased by the strong sea breeze always enjoyed at this place. The wind would hardly suffer one to sit still in the passages. I thought it would give us colds, but they said no, it never happened, & I felt myself grow strong under its influence.

I found with Mrs. Phelps, my two nieces as blooming as Hebes.[29] No northern girls could boast a purer white, or more delicate cheeks. Something for the climate after 3 years residence, with many & peculiar troubles.

Mr. Jamison,[30] an intelligent young lawyer, once a student of Transylvania, Kentucky, resides with Dr. Phelps.

A town is laid out at this place, called Orizembo,[31] & lots offered for sale. It numbers but two houses, that of Dr. Phelps & one other.

5. Orizimbo Plantation, home of Dr. James Aeneas E. Phelps. The house once served as a prison for Santa Anna. [by Don Hudson, courtesy of Dow Chemical.]

OPPOSITE
4. "Dr. Phelps' house on the prairie—from recollection." (For information on the Phelps family see Note #28.)

The next league, also held by Mrs. Alsbury has its town—called Montezuma.[32] The rage is now for making towns. At the period of my former visit, nobody thought of more than individual improvements, now all are for speculation. An unfavorable change—the source of innumerable rivalries affecting the harmony of society.

After breakfast passing by a winding way, under innumerable natural arches through the woodland of Dr. Phelps, we reached the rivers bank & crossed in our own boat to Bolivar, where, but for fatigue, I should have arrived last night. My 3 little nephews were all to receive us.

If my friends were glad to see me they were not more happy than I to reach my home.

But this place is not without painful associations. Here was the scene of my labors & hopes. Here the roses were as formerly blooming & the garden smiling, but here had perished two loved ones—victims of that dreadful year of flood & cholera. The two Marys[33] *were not.*

May 13th

Thursday
Brother started for St. Filipi on important business.

14th

Thermometer 86° at noon. Dr. Hawley & Mr. Trendale arrived while we were at supper—glad to see them—walked in the garden long & talked about Texas & its prospects.

15th

Walked about the place in search of the great live oaks so much talked of. Did not find but one—a bee tree[34]—had been girdled & stript of its leaves to my sorrow—what wanton barbarism. Discovered the little burying ground with roses blooming on two fresh graves—dropped there a tear—had dreaded to inquire for them. It is well chosen—a little enclosure—figs & growing luxuriantly without & flowers blooming within.

10 o'clock

Thermometer at 86, fresh sea breeze—accompanied the gentlemen across the river & through the avenue to Dr. Phelps's—a charming walk—the high trees protecting from the sun—the blackberries refreshing us with their tempting fruit—very sweet & abundant—they led their horses, which were in waiting at the bank—all of us preferring to walk. By way of experiment I mounted one of their Spanish saddles for a short distance.

From Bolivar to Orizymbo—about ¾ of a mile through woodland very much like the shrubbery of Col. Perkins & Mr. Bussey[35] near Boston though on a far grander scale.

In the corridor of Dr. Phelps we inhaled with a sensation of delight the sea breezes[36] over the prairie over which the eye extends 9 miles. In the distance are two wooded points resembling the narrows below N York, & you fancy the sea beyond. One would think that nothing but health could be borne on such gales, for they are fresh & strong, yet Mrs. Phelps was lying ill of scarlet fever, from which several members of her family had but recently recovered. This led to various speculations on epidemic disease. What region escapes entirely? Is it that we need not *forget our mortality*? In such a position one feels such perfect contentment there is danger of doing so.

After partaking of a family dinner,[37] consisting of rabbit soup—a piece of yankee pickled pork—venison steaks—with snap beans—remarkably fine Irish potatoes & lettuce from the garden—our visitors took leave for Columbia very favorably impressed with this episode from their *grand tour* through the colony. I turned my steps homeward accompanied by Mr. Jamison with his gun, which he had occasion to exercise on the squirrels, *en passant,* while I partook of the blackberries. One fine fellow received his death wound through the eye by the Kentucker & was deposited in the skiff for my supper.

We learned that a Mexican Cutter has captured a Schooner supposed to have contraband goods off Velasco.[38] The passengers, among them Mr. McKinny the owner, being put on shore. The schooner had Mexican colours. So much for disregarding all laws on the ground that there is not power to enforce them.

The Texas people are ungrateful to Mexico to whom they owe so much. Not satisfied with very lenient laws they evade all law. How can they be made to respect it? Mr. McKinny is charged with smuggling.[39]

May 16th

Thermometer 82° at noon.

17th

81°

18th

82°

19th

morning—80° 9 A.M. o'clock.   noon—86°—6 P.M.—80°.

20th

9 A.M.—80°.   noon—86°.   6 P.M. 80°.

21st

9 A.M.—80°.   Noon—83°.
A strong sea breeze at this time—no rain.
Brother returned from San Filipe with a dislocated shoulder—having been thrown by a vicious Mustang he hired to relieve his own faithful Ball, getting tired.

22nd

9 A.M.—80°—noon—82°. Had for dinner this day a large soft shell turtle from the river—have fish, crabs, shrimps & crawfish any day for the taking.[40]

23rd

9 A.M.—80°.
Brother started for Brazoria to make arrangements for our passage for N.O. I wrote to daughter[41] & Mr. Buddington.
noon—85°. rattle snake killed in the yard.

24th

Sunday
9 A.M.—79°.   noon—83°.   6 P.M.—80.
Dined this day at Dr. Phelps. Dr. Pollard[42] there. Heard rattle snakes hissing all night.[43]

May 25th

9 A.M.—79° SW. A few drops rain—2 or 3 times this morning—not enough to wet the ground—sunshine between—noon—82° SE. Mrs. Phelps dined with us. 6 P.M.—81 SE.

26th

6 A.M.—76° SW.
9 A.M.—82° SE.
noon—84° SE.
6 P.M.—82 SE.
Brother returned from Brazoria.

27th

9 A.M.—80°
noon—86°
6 P.M.—82°

28th

9 A.M.—80°
noon—86°
6 P.M.—82°

May 29th

9 A.M.—78°
noon—86°
6 P.M.—82°

30th

9 A.M.—79°
noon—85°
6 P.M.—80°

31st

8 A.M. cloudy—80°   S.E.
noon clear—85°   S.E.
6 P.M. clear—82°   S.E.

June 1st

6 A.M. cloudy—78°	S.
noon, showery—82°	S.E.
shower of 10 minutes,	E.
another shower	
6 P.M. clear. 76°	E.

Rained violently all night with thunder and lightning.

2nd

6 A.M.—72°	S.W.
noon cloudy—82°	S.E.
6 P.M. clear—80°	S.E.

June 3rd

6 A.M. clear—72°	S.W.
noon clear—86°	S.E.
6 P.M. clear—84°	S.E.

4th

6 A.M. clear—74°	S.E.
noon clear—85°	S.E.
6 P.M. clear—84°	S.E.

5th

6 A.M. few clouds—72°	S.W.
noon clear—85°	S.E.
6 P.M. clear—82°	S.E.

6th

6 A.M. cloudy—78°	S.
noon clear—86°	S.
6 P.M. rainy—82°	S.E.[44]

Tuesday

Start for Brazoria in a perogue. Could not accomplish my objects by staying longer. No way to travel about or to remove to the coast—staying at Bolivar through the summer dangerous to health. The rich bottom lands in Texas, as in other warm countries engender miasmata. Brother desires to send his children to Kentucky. Give up my own views to accommodate him, & through necessity. Mortifying not to see more of the country after all my trouble. Can't help it, want the children to have the benefit of the trip—will not cost more or so much as living here with bad management.[45]

noon—Touched at Bell's landing to search for my lost things—not to be found. Looks busy there, a large new ware house full of things & people. Schooner San Iago[46] loading with cotton lying here was set on fire last night—much damaged— cotton bales, in all stages of destruction lay every where in melancholy confusion. Nearly all the way to Brazoria—where cotton black & white covered half the surface of the river—amused ourselves with gathering some.

Our oarsmen very lazy—Did not arrive till midnight—Every body asleep—Silent as death—Called up Mr. & Mrs. Andrews—The air was very chilly—I felt sick from exposure—Waked in the morning with head ache—staid all day to get better—did not enjoy anything—Young ladies occupied with company—Some genteel looking young men here—got up a little ball for Miss Austins—I could not go—Tried to refresh my self with sleep. Could not close my eyes—heard music & dancing—singing—hollowing till morning—rose before the sun to proceed *en voyage*.

June 8th

Saw Dr. & Mrs. Applewhite[47] had much conversation with them on the prospects of the country.

Landed at noon at a new place just opened by Mr. Crosby[48] near the bank—The trees are so thinned you can see through the timber to the prairie in beautiful vistas. Longed to have time to explore a little. Mrs. Perry[49] lives but two miles off, yet I can not get to see her—nor can I visit my 200 acres[50] near by, must proceed—may lose passage—must go soon if at all.

Moved on most tediously—were out all night—felt very sick

June 10th

at daylight moored along side San Filipe—glad enough to get to my old quarters. Lady passengers Mrs. Sayre[51] & Mrs. Porter.

Got arranged & felt somewhat rested through the day—The fine sea breeze invigorates—Had prospect of a wind 2 or 3 times—file in to the stream to be ready for the first fair breeze—along side of the Julius Ceasar—also waiting full of passengers.

6. Probably the farm of "Old Rock," described in the diary entry for April 7, 1838. On this farm, Mary Austin Holley saw another side of early Texas life.

Some ladies were here for benefit of sea air—Miss McNeal[52]—Miss Lowe[53] & others—came on board.

They ride on the beach & bathe in the surf as at Nahant and Long Branch. The breakers roar as loud as at Niagara Falls.

The moon was full—rising over the sea—The fishermen in their red shirts hauled in their last nets—all objects stood out in full relief—Velasco[54] with its many hovels —huts—boarding houses & signal staffs—on the left—McKenney's house—warehouse—cotton gin & camp of newly landed Africans[55]—on the right herds of cattle & horses feeding as far off as eye could reach—people lounging or busy every where. The wide prairie, through which the smooth Brazos rolls—the noisy sea before, skiffs & sail boats with the light canoes shooting over the surface in every direction— all these objects—all pretty in the distance—formed a picturesque whole.

While I was making a sketch of Velasco, & before I had finished the sail boat just hoisting sail, she shot off from the shore & was along side with a party of ladies & gentlemen to take Mr. Sayre for a riding party on the beach by moon light. The rest of us remained on deck talking & singing glees, duets & solos for some hours. I took my guitar—it is always a resource at such moments. I sang Pensez à moi[56] & other songs. Capt. Hutton of the Julius Ceasar knows Mr. Drake—promises me the music of his other songs in possession of his sister & cousin at Pensecola.

June 11th

Thanks to *Dr. Cook* feel very well this morning. Cook's Pills are worth all the Seidlitzs & every thing else—

Still waiting for a wind. Captains Hurd & Hutton[57] are taking observations—

Latitude	29°
Longitude	95°
Temperature noon	82°
Wind—strong	53

Take fish as fast as the line is thrown in. Crabs are large & fine. Find it very agreeable being here—as good for health as any sea shore—grow strong every minute.

News came of the death of Miss Fuller sister of Capt. Fuller[58] a fine rosy cheeked girl—at McNeals—fever—

Reading life of Mrs. Siddons[59]—an interesting book—

12th

Morning   80°. Fine sheepshead for breakfast—

Feel very well—sit all day on the deck, gazing on the ridge of white breakers & the beautiful blue sea beyond.

Count 4 wrecks in the view—The Elizabeth nearly in pieces, lies on the point of Velasco. It is but a month since she was proudly entering the river behind the San

Felipe. Dr. Applewhite & family were on board.

The long prevalence of southerly winds has rendered this bad bar almost impassable.

| noon | 84° |
| Evening | 82 |

20th

| Morning | 84° |
| noon | 86 |

Mrs. Perry,[60] sister of Col. Austin, hearing of my being at the mouth came down with her husband to see me—was at Mrs. McKennys. Mrs. Perry came for us in a boat & we all went ashore to see her. Spent the evening in conversation about her brother & family & other interesting topics after which enjoyed a walk along the beach & came on board.

Mean time Captains of San Felipe & Julius Ceasar agreed should it be calm in the morning to force a passage over the bar & in case one vessel stuck fast, the other should take the passengers & proceed.

13th

Daylight was an interesting moment—instead of calm a light northern breeze sprang up—The Julius Ceasar, being of lightest draft went first—all sail hoisted—both vessels went proudly out to sea—the Brig Durango followed. It was a day of rejoicing to all concerned.

Happy are those who are not subject to sea sickness.[61] I am not of the happy number—all was misery to me. I took to my berth & there I lay 5 days—the heat intolerable—I seemed to be in my coffin without power to move—literally stewed—rejecting all I swallowed. Mrs. Sayre lay opposite to me in the same predicament all our comfort was in seeing which could groan the loudest.

We had very light breezes & for 2 days & then a calm 4 successive days. If a wind sprung up at night & we made a little head way, we fell back in the day by the current—our vessel seemed like the specter ship—always tugging & never moving. Having no motion we recovered from our sickness, but the heat & the calm was as bad, tedious beyond every thing. The deep blue sea was one vast mirror. I could not stand till I had a salt bath fixed—baths twice a day gave me some vigour. I could then loll on the deck under the awning & watch the flabby sails—& sing feebly to the guitar when the sun had gone down. What a luxury were those baths! All lay helter skelter on the deck—some were feverish. One I thought would die. In moments of delirium he would stalk about the vessel like a spectre.

We had 276 bales of cotton, placed wherever they could be—interrupting a free current of air—when air there was. We had but salt provisions & bad water & a scarcity of both—mutinous sailors, with a prospect of a protracted voyage. At last, after seven days—seeming as many years—the Balize lights[62] hove in sight. What joy—what life—those only who have experienced a calm at sea can know. I was always on deck at the first dawning light, to see the sun rise from the ocean & to catch a wholesome breath. How glorious was the morning!

The steamer Porpoise took us in tow with the Julius Ceasar just behind & 3 others. We were lashed to her lee side just opposite the boiler with the smoke & steam added to that of our own caboose. Thus we proceeded for 2 whole days at a snail's pace. It was uncomfortable enough & there seemed no end to our petty annoyances. One night it rained hard, the Cabin leaked, we were wet to the skin in our berths & every where, & the mosquitoes devoured us.

7. "Plantation of Mr. Sayre on the Brazos, 40 miles from the sea. ½ league. This house, 56 by 40, cost from $800 to 1000. . . ."

We did however arrive on the night of the 22nd 9 o'clock. Put ashore in the yawl, the whole party streaked straight for a *soda shop*[63] the place of our fondest anticipation for many days. No topers were ever so happy as we.

Proceeded to St. Peters St.[64] found nobody but the servants. Took possession of the spacious rooms & beds & comforts so grateful to the weary & worn out.

My *second Impressions* of Texas not half so agreeable as the *First*.[65]

June 23rd

1835

New Orleans—

Passed a few hot, sickly disagreeable days in N. Orleans—Family Labranche all away—my friends, Maramand [?], Schricker, Frederic—as ever, Kind. Kept my bed a day & had a Doctor—thought I was getting a fever—glad to get a passage in the Junius for Louisville.

June 29th

Monday Evening—Mr. Frederick & Mr. Budington saw us on board. Mr. and Mrs. Sayre fellow passengers.

Boat small, but comfortable. Shakes a great deal. Fear 'twill injure my piano. I got in N. O. Dislike a shaking boat.

July 3rd

A very fine morning—stopped at Nactchez before day. Full of the pleasant recollections with which I landed there with my husband in 1827. I persuaded the ladies to take a walk to view the place. Returned almost in disgust. Did not strike us agreeably.[66]

Learned here that the plantation of Stafford[67] just above Bolivar was sold yesterday to Mr. Neal of Natches—including 20 negroes & stock (50,000 head worth $4,000) for $42,000.

People on the way inquire eagerly about Texas.

Mr. Sayre[68] purchased his plantation—a ½ league of Old Baily—for $500.

Old Baily was a Kentuckian.[69] Went to Texas in the early settlement of the Colony & fixed himself in that choice solitary spot, when there was scarce a settlement on the Brazos. Here, with his wife & children, he resided in peace and was getting things snug and comfortable around him till evil-tongued rumor dragged him from his retreat.

Word came to Col. Austin that Baily had been a convict in the penetentiary of Kentucky. He, bound for the good character of the colonists, sent forth an order, as was his custom in such cases to decamp within 3 days on pain of summary punishment. Baily replied that true he had been in the penetentiary, & also he had been in The Legislature of Kentucky, where he opposed the manufacture of so many Banks by which he & so many others had been ruined. Upon which he had been tempted to the crime of forgery—or to do that on a small scale which they had been doing on a great one. He had paid the forfeit—had stolen off to his present retreat to lead an honest & solitary life—far from the world—which he desired neither to injure or to serve & wished but to be let alone.

Upon this Col. Austin paid him a visit & was so well pleased with the conversation & improving condition of the old man & his family that he left him to live & die in peace.

The cholera in 1832 finished his career. He died in Brazoria where it cannot be said he *lies interred* for he was buried *erect* & in full dress according to his desire.

The mimosa is a very general & very beautiful plant in Texas, forming in many places a thick carpet. One hates to tread upon its shrinking leaves & its delicate blue flowers as common as the grass. I have observed it on the river's bank growing to the water's edge making to the eye a most tempting seat. Nothing could be prettier.

"We were overshadowed by lofty trees with straight smooth trunks, like stately columns & as the glowing rays of the sun shone through the transparent leaves tinted with the many colored hues of autumn, I was reminded of the effect of sunshine among the stained windows & clustering columns of a Gothic cathedral. Indeed, there is a grandeur & solemnity in some of our spacious forests of the west that awaken in me the same feeling that I have experienced in those vast & venerable piles, & the sound of the wind sweeping through them supplies, occasionally the deep breathings of the organ."—Irving's Tour on the Prairies[70]

"The Bay of Espiritu Santo[71] is the next harbor of importance, & this from the frequency of shoals can not be frequented by vessels drawing more than 8 or 10 feet of water"—Sketch of Texas in *"Atkinsons casket"*[72]

List of Articles given for Kentucky Emigrants[73]

April 25

Mr. Thomas Hunt	1 Piece vesting
Mr. Collins	1 piece shirting
Mr. Henry	6 yds. linen on spool thread
Mr. Shwet [?]	[?] 000
Mr. Hale	striped stuff for pantaloons
Thilford [?] & Holloway	0
Rainey & Ferguson	0

Leavy & Dolen
Robinson   30 yrds. cotton, thread & buttons
Morrison & Hunter   0
Iles & Wright   vesting—cotton—su [?]
McKinney   0
Mr. North   4 vests—cut 25 vests
Mr. Brand   piece check for hunting shirts

1837

Novr 27th

Cash a/ct	Dr.
Balance due on bill	25.00
To proceeds of note for $1000	979.31

Dec. 12th

to proceeds of book sold at Vicksburg by Wm. Smedes [?]	$30
Cash	Cr.

Nov. 27th

Frazer's bill	$	6.50
Bonsets for young Carlos		8
Mrs. Ross for Mary		50
To Horace		22
Frazer's bill		28.82
Hale & Hunter do		24.89

28th

North's do	15.25
Mrs. Hunter for dresses	8
Mrs. green do	1.75

29th

Expenses to Louisville	18.25

Dr. [?] Smith for boys   69
Shoes & gloves   5
                           ──────────────
                           $ 257.46[74]

                           Dec.

Expenses to N. O.
[?] bought in N. O.
Expenses to Galveston
Crackers & Cheese[75] $ 13
Expenses to Houston
            to Brazoria

                           1837

                           Dec. 6

Left Louisville. Steamboat Henry Clay—Holton

                           13th

Arrived N.O.

                           15th

Left N. O.   Columbia

                           18th

Arr'd Galveston

                           20th

Left   do   S. Huster[?]

                           22nd

Arr[d] Houston—Camenche[?]

The Texas Diary, 1835–38

Cold—weather, fair

Attended church at the capital. Visited Gallery[76] of paintings with the President.[77] Express arrived saying the Enemy (1500) had then taken possession of Bexar & one small force there under Col. Carnes.[78]

No Christmas merry making all busy with preparations for war.

Camenche left—went to Mrs. Allens[79] to dine—after called on Mr. Labranche[80] American Minister who returned & passed the evening with us. Mr. Kerr—secretary of Legation—& other company. Public meetings were held to provide means for meeting the enemy—$5000 subscribed—much patriotism displayed—a sailor gave $80, silver, all he had. The President had no time to eat his dinner—seldom has. Lives next to Mrs. Allen's—his house has one room[81]—always crowded with persons on business. When wearied past endurance he goes out & sits down on the prairie back of the carbin which makes his *palace*. A better house is building. Weather clear and mild with gusts. Staid all night with Mrs. Allen—very hospitably entertained— a new good house—well—even elegantly furnished. Weather clear. Mrs. McCormack[82] owns the Battle ground-house on the hill.

Galveston to	
Dollar Point	12 miles
Mouth of Dickson	
Edwards Point	12 miles
Clappers Point	15 miles
Harrisburgh	15
Houston	6 miles
Houses in Houston	200
Laid out (Mr. Allen) Jan., 1836	
Width Buffalo Bayou at its mouth	120 yds
from Harrisburgh to Houston average	80 feet
at Harrisburgh Bray's Bayou	
at Houston White Oak Bayou[83]	
Carpenter's wages $5 to 10 per/day	
Eggs 3 to 6 $ per doz.	
Sperm candles 50cts each	
Butter $1.25 lb	
Sugar 75cts.[84]	

The houses in Houston are chiefly in the margin of the timber line, on the Bayou. A fine prairie extends back & some of the best situations are scattered over it from which you view in the distance whatever is going on. The Capitol stands in the prairie making a good appearance—was built by Mr. Allen—cost 30,000$—rents for $5000 —a block of 11 stores also built by Mr. Allen—cost $12,000—rent from $500 to $700 each.[85]

Houston is not healthy—several bilious cases exist at present—contains 1500 to 2,000 inhabitants. 80 sailors are now in Houston. The houses generally are of 1 story a few have 2. 2 large hotels with galleries above & below.

Dec. 26th

600 to 700 men militia were enrolled for service this day—citizens—¾ young men. $2000 subscribed. A vessel bought for $8000. Capt. Wheelright[86] to command. In town meeting it was agreed to pursue the enemy even to the City of Mexico.

Thermometer 65°—sit with doors & windows open.

Rode out to Gen. Bakers.[87] 2½ miles from town.

Visited Mrs. Bee[88]—the family much affected by the death of a little daughter with sore throat.

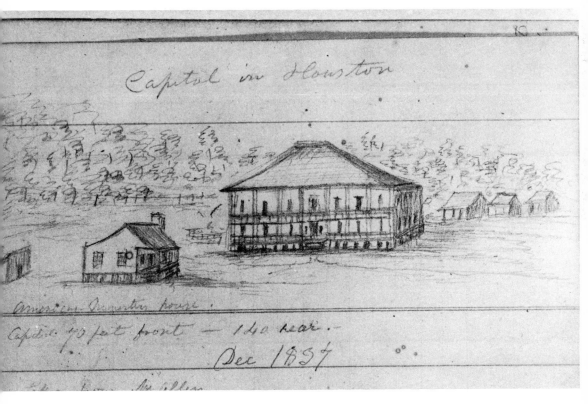

8. "Capitol in Houston, December 1837, taken from Mrs. Allen's. Capitol 70 feet front, 140 in rear. [Also depicted is the] American legation house." This sketch is probably the oldest facsimile of the first capitol.

9. "Houston contains three hundred houses, first house built in Jany. 1836. [Also shown in the sketch is the house of] Felix Houston [*sic*]." The Allen brothers named their settlement after Sam Houston even before he had been elected President.

Mr. Allen and Mr. [?Menard] on horseback with white plumes.

President ill all this day. Could hear him groan all night. Unfit for business. Good laborers can get any wages—a cook $50 per month. A block of stores (11) in main street cost 12000—rent from $500 to 700—one store in same street, 2 stories—painted white cost $10,000.

Judge Birdsall—Attorney General—from N. York knows Myron & Orville Holley.[89] Said reading my book a year since brought him here. Is a youthful—handsome man.

The President's cabin has no glass—slats across the windows with blankets interwoven supply the place.

A volunteer company is organizing.

Col. Morehouses's[90] command of the regular army (80 men) start tomorrow.

A committee of vigilance appointed. Citizens subscribed liberally.

all is busy with preparation & the note of war.

Hear the howling of wolves at night.

No garden in Houston—none but imported vegetables.

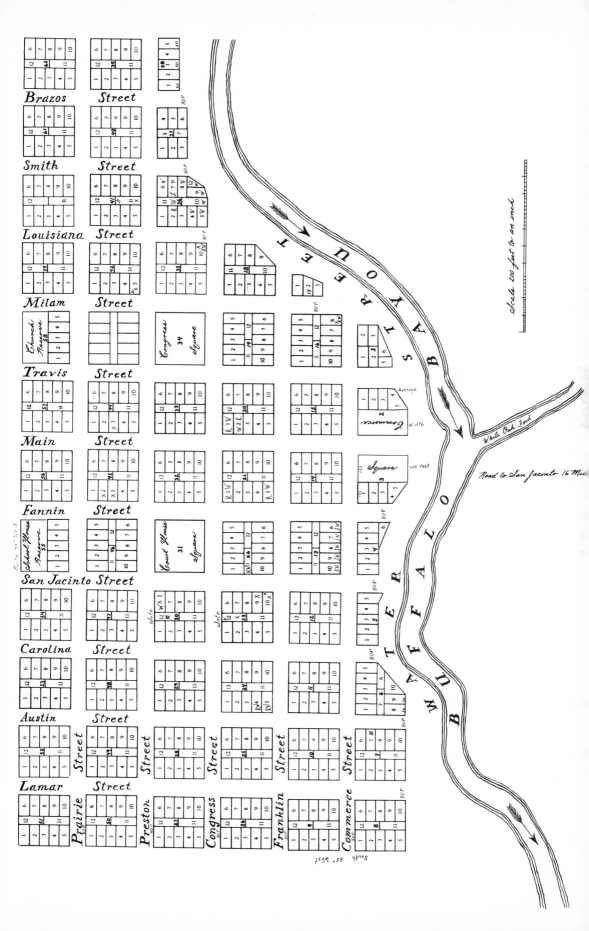

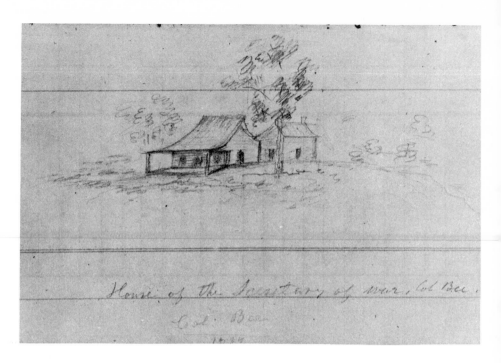

10a. "House of the Secretary of War, Col. Bee, 1837."

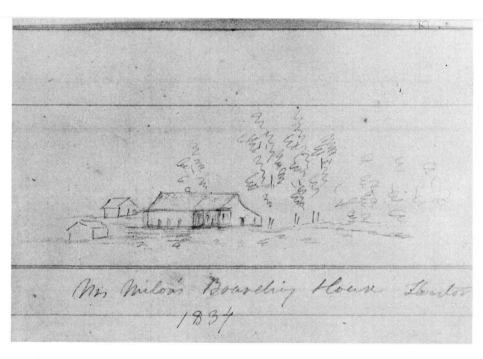

10b. "Mrs. Milon's boarding house, Houston, 1837."

Thermometer (9 o'clock) 67°—weather clear.

Just a month since we left Lexington. Have not had a rainy day; nor one instance of ill luck. Gen. Baker issued militia orders.

Start for Brazoria in a return Barouche—with baggage wagon—gentlemen on horseback—Feel remarkably well—good appetite—good digestion.

Summer heat.

Travel through prairie, by points of timber—on the south nothing but the horizon to bound the view. Seems to me beautiful even in winter, no flowers, & most of the prairie burnt over—much of the timber is evergreen—mixed with grey. Land not very good along here—roads want but to be travelled more to be excellent—a little wet in low places—wants to be ditched.[91]

Passed clear lake[92]—a beautiful spot—surrounded by timber—too much moss on the trees for health—a desserted house stands on the margin under some fine oaks. The people who lived here were healthy, Mr. B. says—

Miss the live oaks on this road—approaching the Brazos they begin to appear.

No dwelling on the road till we reach Bingham[93]—30 miles from Houston.

Took us from 11 to 6 without stopping—an agreeable ride without fatigue. Saw deer & abundance of cranes. Bingham house better than the common run of taverns in Kentucky.

Had a good supper—good beds at Mr. Binghams & breakfast—price—$2.50 each. Mr. B. has had sickness in his family the past season—the first time & he has made 9 crops here.

15 persons lodged here.

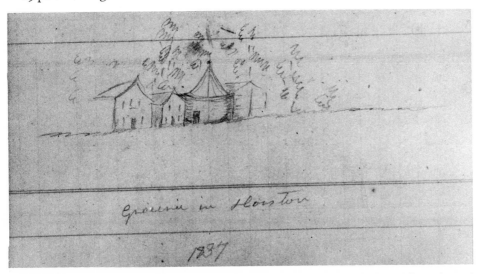

11. "Grocerie in Houston, 1837." This appears to be Kesler's Round Tent Saloon, located between Franklin and Congress Avenues. The term "Grocerie" was a nineteenth century colloquialism for tavern or saloon.

Waked by the birds—the beautiful red birds—great numbers with their scarlet crests were in the garden & yard. Morning foggy.

Start refreshed—escorted by Colonels & Captains on their way to the seat of war in advance of the army.

The sun shone out—summer heat—*Cavalry* complacent—prospect improves—fine timber houses frequent—between every point of timber.

Saw an immense flock of wild geese on the ground. They suffered us to pass without alarm. Saw ladies walking in the prairie. Passed fine fields of cotton & corn & good looking houses, one painted white, 2 stories high, stood beautifully among high live oaks.[94]

For more than 10 miles our course was due east—following the points of timber—then south. A road in a line from the Brazos to Houston would be much shorter & with bridges & ditches would be the finest in the world. On either side but our right, where lay the timber, the prairie stretched out to that extent that you seemed to look up hill from the rotundity of the Earth. We saw horsemen like specks in the distance in fact men as far as the eye could reach—such distance, like the ocean, is sublime. Some prairies which had been burnt over were springing with new grass like a field of grain.

Saw a chase between a white headed eagle & a wild goose he selected from a flock. He pursued it long in various gyrations high above our heads & near the earth, at times almost fixing his talons in the frantic screaming bird, when with redoubled strength the goose would make a new turn & evade his mortal enemy. At last the suffering animal regained the agitated flock & the eagle abandoned his prey.

Approaching Brazoria the live oaks are truly magnificent. A house any where in the verge of the timber would make a paradise. One is struck with the infinite superiority in beauty & fertility of this region to the neighborhood of Houston.[95]

Brazoria—our escort, Colonels Morehouse, Fisher, Captain Todd[96]

Arrived at 7 in Brazoria. Found a kind welcome with Mr. & Mrs. Andrews.[97]

Brazoria

Dec. 29th

Morning bright. Air vocal with the music of red birds & others. Gathered a rose from the garden—where are orange trees of good size, but not yet bearing.

Fixed off Col. Morehouse with needles, thread, etc., for the frontier. Expects his company will overtake him in Texana on the Navidad.[98] Fears the detachment under Col. Seguin[99] has been cut off by the enemy.

Edward's Point[100] was sold yesterday for 28,000$—¼ resold for $10,000.

Mr. Sayre[101] made 75 bales cotton this year—12 hands—the gale injured the crop half.

Militia organizing all over the country. A company started from Columbia this day. Some companies from Colorado have been in the field some days

No preparation, or orders from government, yet. Were warned of the danger by a message from U. S. Sloop of War some time since.

Visit from Gen. Lamar[102] & Col. Somerville.[103] Both pressing for head quarters. Gen. Lamar has no time for the memoirs of Gen. Austin. Proposed to give me the materials he has collected.

Dec. 30th

Bright morning with summer heat.

Went out to shoot at a mark with a rifle—Capt. Labranche our teacher—fired 3 rounds each—had much amusement—drank 2 bottles champagne, with cakes at Mrs. Blandins[104]—at whose house we were—formerly John Austin's home where I staid in 1831—& where I planted the first strawberries in Texas. The place much improved—shrubbery, orange rose &c, much grown.

Rode out on horse back after dinner.

Brother Henry[105] arrived.

A traveller from the West reports the Enemy in large force on San Antonio.

Celebrated New Year's Eve with a supper—present some young ladies & gentlemen. Drank champagne[106]—sung & danced in the New Year.

Weather so warm no need of fire. Fig trees budding—some talk of gardening.

Table always set in an open gallery with curtains.

There were white frost[107] & thin ice about Christmas. The Thermometer once fell as low as 29° in Houston. A norther, of some days duration before we arrived & just after.

1838

Jan. 1st

A lovelier morning never shone.

Spent the day chiefly in conversation with brother on business. Weather like summer all day—windows & doors open—grass like young wheat—fig trees budding—talk of gardening. Evening company & music—serenade—robbery.

2nd

Proposed a ride to Bailey's Prairie, across the river, on horseback, after starting grew very warm with light clouds & misty. Talked of returned—persevered—sun shone out—had a charming day. Could not be a pleasanter ride through the wood &

prairie. Called at the house of Mrs. Polley—3 miles—treated with madeira—smugled—invited to dinner. Mounted & rode on to Mrs. Bowen's[108]—a widow—4 miles. A very handsome black eyed lady—young—3 handsome children. Cotton field back of the house—had done picking—yet it was white with cotton. Longed to gather it—said it would not pay the expense of further labor. Returning to Polley's Mrs. Andrews horse ran away with her—frightened us much. Went like lightening to the gate & stopped suddenly—she slipped off, almost fainting—Gilpin like.[109]

Had an excellent dinner of chicken—biscuit—coffee, &c.

Mrs. Polley is the daughter of *old Bailey*—hence the name of the prairie—cotton farms are nearly contiguous along the edge of the prairie. Some fine situations, belonging to the Hawkins[110] estate, remain to be cultivated.

Got home just after sun set charmed with our excursion.

In our absence had been discovered that some young men, before respectable, had been concerned in carrying off a trunk of money from the store of Mr. Blandin during a serenade for our benefit on the 1st in which Mr. Brewer the head clerk, was occupied.

Frazer—an under Clerk of 16 (a New Yorker) confessed he had been bribed to hand out the trunk to Mr. Mackey (a Philadelphian) & another person. On examination before the mayor were committed to prison, in irons, the night.

Miserable infatuation that could lead young men to such self sacrifice for a few hundred dollars when so many roads to wealth are open in Texas. Onderdonk is here.

Gen. Lamar passed the morning with us. Is very taciturn—when he does speak it is in wit or poetry in compliment. He is rather under size—thick set—rosy cheeks—highforehead—hair parted—speaks very slow[111]—staid a good while & went out with—"Too late I staid, forgive the crime," &c.

Says the Archives of the state at Monteray containing documents pertaining to the early history of Texas may be obtained by a small sum of money.

Jan. 3rd

Warm morning with light clouds & wind. Sunshine by fits. Fire-board put up as in summer. The yard full of red birds.

The climate answers well to my description—perpetual summer—altho' during the norther Mr. Labranche complained I had deceived him into the imprudence of bringing neither blanket nor cloak & he had suffered. In all climates there is occasional need of these articles.

Mr. Andrews made hay of prairie grass for experiment—found it excellent for horses & cows who liked it.

The Cushattue Indians[112] come to Bolivar to protect it in times of danger, from friendly feelings.

Brazoria has not grown much since I was here. It is now made the county seat again[113] and will probably take a start.

Mr. Durier from the Bernard called in one day—had his house burned by the enemy during the war, his negroes carried off, & being discouraged is about to quit the country.

Col. Love[114] returned from Velasco—is much pleased there—means to purchase. About noon set on to rain. Prevents Brother going home—rain all night.

Jan. 4th

Warm & rainy. Cleared up at noon with a norther—had a good fire all the evening —cold night.

Col. Love went to Columbia after dining with us.

Jan. 5th

Bright, clear, warm morning.

After dinner started for Peach Point[115] on horseback—road led through a wood of Holly & peach—took a nearer path where immense live oaks meet at top forming a canopy through long vistas fit for the residence of Druids—like scenes in Norma.[116]

Reached Mrs. Perry's (12 miles),[117] at sundown.

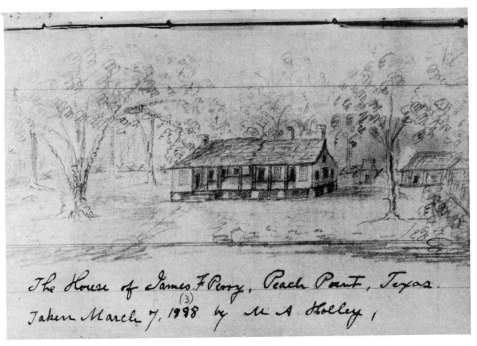

12. "The house of James F. Perry, Peach Point, Texas. Taken March 7, 1838, by M. A. Holley."

13. A ferrotype of Peach Point Plantation, ca. 1840, home of James F. Perry, courtesy of the Bryan family. Two rooms at the front left quartered Stephen F. Austin's study and bedroom. See notes on Fig 13.

Jan. 6th

Warm, but damp, a fire pleasant. Some gardens made & peas up in this neighborhood. Radishes & lettuce on the table—large & excellent.

Could view the Gulf 8 miles distant, if the house was high enough.[118]

The horizon bounds the prospect in one direction, the timber of the Bernard on the other, a fine forest back between it & the Brazos.

This situation has no fault but that it seems low & you look up hill.[119] A spreading live oak overshadows the house, which is 1 story, a double cabin.

Onions in the garden some inches high.

MARY AUSTIN HOLLEY

Jan 7th

Warm & rainy & so calm you hear the roar of the breakers like distant thunder.
Generally it is windy on the prairies.

A large tree here & there in the prairie looks like a vessel under sail.

Clear at noon.

Mr. Baird[120] is staying at Mr. Perry's. He came to Texas with cousin Stephen in 1821 by land & tells us many anecdotes of that period.

He was one of the first company of young men who engaged to come to Texas with cousin Moses & had started at the time of his death. He joined Stephen in N. Orleans & together with the following young men:

October 1821

William Little
————— Marshall
Edward Lovelace
Henry Holson
Samuel Fay
Joseph Polley
Edward Barr
————— Higginbottom
John Morse
Benjamin Ballou
Lt. Barnum
Lt. Wilson
Dr. James Hewetson[121] .

and accompanied by
————— Seguin
————— Berrmendi,[122] Mexican officers, they proceeded by Natchitoches to San Antonio, there they obtained a surveyor & visited Matagorda Bay, crossed over to the Brazos—exploring and survaying the country. They returned to N Orleans by the road they came.

Dec. 1821

Jonah Bell—Abner Keykendal—Robinson & Gates—preceded a little Gen. Austin, & built a cabin at Labadie—now Washington.[123]

An arrangement was made with Jos. Hawkins to fit out a vessel to the Colorado with provisions while Gen. A. went on by land to meet them. In the vessel—the Schooner Lively—[124]returned Baird, the Holtons, Little & Marshall—the others joined afterwards.

They anchored at Galveston Bay for some time—& went on to the Brazos. The Capt. of the Lively insisted it was the Colorado—loitered away his time—consumed his provisions & refused to go farther, thus through his perverseness the benefit of the expedition was lost. At the mouth of the Colorado Gen. Austin with Austin Elliott & one other waited in vain for companions & food.

Dec. 20 [1821]

Baird & his companions landed & wandered about the Brazos—living by the guns —having nothing else. The Capt. refused them any corn for seed—the few grains they had planted at Bell's Landing where they eat roasting ears some time after.

They proceeded to Fort Bend[125] where was commenced the first settlement.

Gen. Austin was forced to go to Mexico.[126]

The Lively returned with some emigrants families & more provisions which through bad management—bad men—or Indians—were wasted. Some emigrants were discouraged & returned—the Indians became troublesome—they had been kept at bay by Long & his party at Galveston.

La Fitte[127] had his headquarters on Galveston Island, where the old custom house stood.

The Lively was lost on her 3rd trip.

In 1812 there was a gale similar to that of 1837.[128] The lower country under water. Timber supposed to have come from the Mississippi was found on Galveston Island. Some logs are now lying in Gulf Prairie supposed to have been washed up at that time. The over flow from the last gale did not reach the Gulf Prairie, nor was the whole of Galveston under water. The sea has receded some distance since the recollection of Mr. Baird.

The schooner Lively made 3 trips. We only saw one.[129]

Jan. 8th

(1838)

Clear, & frosty morning. Wind north—noon clear bright—good fire at night. Columbia at Velasco.

9th

Morning cloudy, wind north—good fire necessary at night. 140 acres—20 hands —Mr. Perry's farm. Mr. Somerville arrived in Columbia.

10th

Morning, cold rainy norther—continued all day.

11th

Clear, cold, wind north.

12th

Clear—cold, with thin ice. Birds singing, notwithstanding.

Mr. Perry returned from Brazoria. Brought letter from Brother John—& newspaper from N. Orleans, no talk of war in them.

13th

Cloudy, mild, southerly wind, gathered boquet of rose buds—never without them.

Jan. 14th

Sunday

Cloudy, very warm, southerly wind, fire scarcely necessary. Blue birds & red birds, martins & mocking birds held a grand oratorio to their Maker this sabath morning.

Mr. McNeal[130] came in to give us the news.

Capt. Carnes is in Houston explains the cause of the war alarm. Rumor came to camp that some hundred of the enemy were approaching—spies did not return—ordered Roderiguez to get his horse ready in case an express should be wanting—he went in search of his horse. They were cleaning & firing the canon of the Fort to be ready, which Roderiguez being at a distance searching for his horse took it for an attack of the enemy & started off, bare back—for Houston. Carnes suspecting this fact, sent some horsemen after him, which he took for the enemy in pursuit, & fled the faster.

Such was the panic. Carnes has been to Mortura[?] no enemy on the road, or preparing to come!

At an election for Clerk, Wm. Wharton[131] presiding, disputed the right of some voters, among them that of an Irishman, a ditcher. "How is this," said the Hibernean, "Col. Wharton? When you were being elected to Congress you said I had a right to vote & made me & the gardener give our votes for you. It is now 6 months since—have I lost any privilege by being so much longer in the country?" The Irish man had been in the employ of Col. Wharton.

Took a walk over the plantation & to the cotton gin. Hate to see so much cotton left in the field. They say it is not worth picking. The stalk is big as a man's head—large as my wrist—the soil quite black—[132]peach land.

The negroes have each a cotton patch—their cotton is ginned after that of their master & sold with his. Some of them make $70 per year. This is the case within all this neighborhood & generally..

The negroes have good cabins & good clothes—2 or 3 suits[133] a year.

Visited the tomb of Gen. Austin.[134] High weeds weep in solitude over it. My poor cousin sleeps in peace.

Have been occupied all this time making notes from family papers & letters in the possession of Mrs. Perry.

Jan. 15th

Monday

Never was a more glorious morning. Air dry & soft. Sun bright. Birds of every hue noisy with music. I walked the gallery an hour before breakfast admiring the beauty of the climate & scene.

Mr. Perry has business up country, as it is called.[135] Proposed at breakfast that his wife & I join him. Agreed.

A summer day—throughout—most charming, gardening.

Mr. Todd called & passed the night—told us of sloop of War Natchez—proposed going to visit her.

Jan. 16th

Morning warm, south east wind. Tremendous thunder storm at noon. Bright afternoon.

17th

Foggy—morning, eveg clear—Dr. Jones[136] came—called in Ned the fiddler & had a little dance in the evening—very warm on going to bed.

18th

A brisk & blustering norther. Sorry I forgot to bring a thermometer to mark these changes—very cold.

A beef was killed from the herd, fed but on grass—very fat—large layers of tallow like stall fed beef. Did not take the trouble to weigh—never saw fatter or more tender beef. All the meats in Texas are tender.[137]

This cold is discouraging for my journey. A norther in the prairie is not an agreeable thing to be caught out in. The wind blows & the rain pours & there is no shelter at hand.

Had a dance tonight to keep warm.

Were to go to a ball in Brazoria yesterday. Weather did not permit.

19th

The coldest weather this year. Ice was formed last night. Clear & cold this morning—gathered a bunch of beautiful roses & buds notwithstanding—a little drooping—the tender leaves of the orange trees look wilted.

20th

Moderate—not warm. The prairie across the Bernard is on fire.[138] The effect tonight is beautiful. Nearly the whole horizon in that direction is a sheet of fire, with an immence body of smoke. One can imagine it to be an irruption of Vesuvius. It is sublime. Lasted 2 or 3 days: only visible at night.

Jan. 21st

Sunday

Clear—still cold, but moderating. Mr. Perry starts today. Too cold for me though the birds will sing & the flowers will blow.

22nd

Fair, but still cold. The day for the Columbia[139] to be at Velasco.

Mrs. Westall[140] & her mother Mrs. Henry came to dinner.

23rd

Cloudy & mild. Picked some fine rose buds. Planting irish potatoes—rather late— Dined in the open air this day gathered beautiful rose buds. Dr. Jones came—danced in the eveg—reels to the fiddle of one of the slaves.

Major Caldwell[141] called this evening. A genteel man. Used to know him in Hopkinsville, Kentucky. Was going with his overseer to drive up some beeves to supply Velasco market. A good business—brings cash. He is wealthy in lands and cattle by marrying the widow Monson[142] of this prairie.

Warm & rainy all day. After dinner Joel Bryan,[143] Mrs. Perry's oldest son, & Dr. Jones started off for company to dance in the Evening. Before they got far the rain poured & we did not think anybody in their senses would come. After dark, & it was very foggy, we heard voices coming over the prairie & in came the gentlemen with Mr. & Mrs. Westall, & Mr. Henry, *dripping*. They had come 1½ miles. We danced till midnight. Those there were not beds for slept on the floor till daylight, when the company went home.

25th

Foggy—warm enough without fire. Birds are singing & hens cackling. When Mrs. Perry returned after the war the house was full of eggs.[144] The hens had taken possession beds, closets, bureaus—every place was a nest.

26th

Started on horseback, with Mrs. Perry, for Quintana. The road lying all through the prairie. It was very wet from late rains & the day was cloudy, still the ride was most charming. I was mounted on Cousin Stephen's favorite pony, a fine ambler & we passed his chosen spot on this Earth, where he & I were to have our paradise— beautiful indeed it is, diversified with copse & lawn; but how changed to me! This lovely tract now belongs to Joel Bryan, an excellent young man, who was our Cavalier.

Jones Creek is the southern boundary of Peach Point, as it is called. Between it & the Gulf, except a labor, including a mound, a gentle slope, to the sea is vacant land. It is entire prairie & therefore has been left unoccupied. It seems to me valuable, being so near the sea, if but for grazing. The mound is a desirable spot, though innocent of any growth but a few scrubby oaks. Like all the mounds of Texas, it is not of Indian origin, but naturally formed, no doubt, by the sea. The ascent on either side is very gradual, & all around it is what is called *hog wallow,* or gentle risings in the earth like waves. How I wished this spot was mine with a fine house & garden on the top.[145] As we approached the same 20 or 30 deer were ranged on its summit, standing in full relief against the sky. Had we been huntsmen what fine sport! As they discovered our approach they commenced a retreat, in single file. Bounding most gracefully. Innumerable cranes,[146] white & brown, were seated in long rows at intervals, or gamboling in the distance filling the air with their discordant screams. Other birds, & immense flocks of ducks were flying or sitting every direction. Along this region the land is sufficiently dry, & all would be with draining.

Between the mound & the sea is another & smaller rising which struck me as very beautiful. Between the two is a charming lake. Fancy is ever ready to embellish these lovely spots, but it is no easy matter to arrange the details of a domicile in Texas.

Jones Creek, some few yards wide, was deep. I could just keep my feet out & my horse made some plunges—they said he sometimes laid down in the water, I did not care for a cold bath, & had to keep my *courage* up, as well as his *nose*. We got thro' well, horses are the best of friends. The head of the lake too is deep, & as the horse leaps out of the water he is so near the perpendicular you are in no danger of being thrown over his head *but on the contrary*.

5 miles of our route was on the beach—hard as a floor—the surf we heard 12 miles distant at our feet. Sea air, the water, & I could not keep my bonnet on my head—was delightful. Our horses snuffed the breeze & went on with great spirit. In summer, how charming.[147]

Reached Mrs. McKennys as they had just dined. Enough left for us. Mr. Toby was there just arrived from N.O. Mr. & Mrs. Williams[148] also. Mr. W. so long associated with Cousin Stephen. Had much conversation on his affairs in the evening. Seems disposed to do justice to his memory.

Mr. W. has brought funds to establish a bank.[149] 2 Schooners were tossing outside of the bar waiting for a fair wind to cross as we arrived.

Jan. 27th

Saturday

Morning too foggy to see the town. Cleared off bright after breakfast. Sun was too hot to walk in. Sat with doors open—went into the warehouse of McKinney & Williams—a spacious place full of goods of every description—N.O. prices.

Mrs. McKenney's garden is all made—potatoes—peas planted—carrots, cabages —cellery growing.[150]

Had for lunch, oysters, very large—even finer than those of Galveston. "I love the sea—the open sea"[151]—I feel all the time as I sit at the open door & gaze on the perpetual blue & listen to the roar of its breakers.

3 deer were brought in last night. Perhaps some of those we saw. We had venison at breakfast & dinner. Nothing could be finer. One need not complain of fare when tables are loaded with venison, oysters, & beef of the finest quality. These meats are exceedingly tender. Smaller game might be had in any quantity, but they do not seem to think it worth the trouble.[152] They live sumptuously here. All foreign things at command. Strong coffee at rising, breakfast, dinner & supper. London ale & champagne common drinks. They have a delicious kind of battercake made of equal parts of cornmeal & rice. Breakfast & supper differ very little from dinner.

We crossed over to Velasco.[153] *Went a shopping* (they have one store), visited the Archer House, a fine hotel. Large 2 story with gallery painted, white, looks well.

Had a commanding view. Met with Gen. Green[154] the master spirit here who attended us in our walk—pointed to the graves of those who fell in the first battle for Independence—Looked at the old fort—the work of the Mexicans—Velasco looks quite like a place.[155] The Quintana[156] side is the highest & driest. Crossed the ferry at sunset. It was lovely. A Schooner under full sail was crossing the bar. A boat load was just landing & many people were on the shore. The vast sea all before us—the scene was lovely. We called at the Hotel in Quintana—a spacious good building & to look at the house of Col. Barrett not yet finished, & walked on to view some town lots. Mrs. Perry promised me one. It is her property. There is considerable building & business going on here. Found my satin dress too warm. Took a shawl on our walk which I had to carry on my arm, & wished I had left at home. Met, in our walk, one gentleman returning from mouth of Bernard where they had been all day eating oysters & fish—galloping all the way on the beach—12 miles.

Jan. 28th

Sunday

Mrs. Jack cured a swelling in her neck by applying led water[157] constantly—It was gone in two days.

Started for home. Mr. Perry arrived from Houston just as we were ready—A fine bright morning thermometer at 65°—Mrs. McKenny accompanied us—crossed to Velasco & came 4 miles, then came Prairie full of mosquitos, to Mr. Jacks[158]—a fine situation on the river, & prairie also, having timber on the north. A bend in the river makes it beautiful. Garden laid out with a glade to water. Mr. McKinny met us here from Houston.

Jan. 29th

Monday

After breakfast left the beautiful place of Mr. Jack for home. Cloudy morning—prairie wet & full of mosquitoes. Passed Mr. Calvert's[159] & Mr. Wharton's. Nothing but mud all the way to the river. Crossed & stopped at Crosby's[160]—genteel people. Mrs. Crosby is from Philadelphia—daughter of Mr. Merry, of the firm of Farmer Draper & Co. Live in a cabin. Got home to dinner. The road this side far better & scenery much finer than the other side of the river.

Have made a circuit of 20 miles—about as much of a journey as Dr. Franklins first jaunt to Philadelphia.

Shall hardly travel further.

1838

Jan. 30th

Warm & foggy.

31st

Foggy morning—cleared up. We went to pass the day with Mrs. Westall—1½ miles had a good dinner & pleasant time. Saw a man sewing like a woman. Found he is a Mexican prisoner—they have three. They are a faithful, quiet people, have a melancholy cast of countenance—exceedingly sallow, with black hair. He of the needle has blue eyes. He was a tailor.[161]

Feb. 1st

Cold & rainy—so much rain is exceedingly unpleasant!

2nd

The month has come in with a tremendous norther—cold in the night—it froze in my room & I freeze today close by the fire.

Feb. 3rd

Norther continues—clear but horribly cold—ice an inch thick. Have to wear my cloak.

Sunday 4th

Nothing to mark the day—but clean sheets & work laid aside. It makes one value the privilege of going to church. Still cold & clear, some neighbors came to dinner—Westals & McNeal's children included—tedious with nothing to do.

5th

Monday
We were to have dined with McNeals—too rainy & cold.

Tuesday

Mild & misty—notwithstanding went to dinner at McNeals—2 miles. The table was spread with a profusion of meats of the country—excellent coffee all in country style. 2 other families were there. House well built of brick. 2 stories—with a wing— floors laid below—only—no plastering—you see the bricks, inside as without— when finished will be about the best in Texas. The whole affair was rather grotesque, but amusing withal.[162]

Evening—whole party adjourned to Mrs. Westalls[163]—to dance reels to 2 discordant violins & a young negro slapping his hands & his sides to keep time instead of a banjo—pretty good burlesque—wished Mr. Macalister had been there. Refreshments waiting. The family wagon brought us home through the mud about 10.

Wednesday, 7th

Warm—unsettled—weather. They brought in a fine buck—a bear was killed yesterday.

Thursday 8th

Cleared off—fair weather at last. Got letters from home.

Friday 9th

Herds of deer were contentedly passing within our view.

Took a ride to mouth of the Bernard in a light wagon—very pleasant over the prairie—12 miles—galloped over the beach, hard as a floor, with great delight. You can ride thus from Matagorda to Galveston, having to cross the mouths of the rivers & bayous.[164] The latter are full of oysters—you can see them in piles above the surface whenever there is mud.

Saturday 10th

Went to dine at Greenville McNeals. On these occasions have to start at 10 or 11 o'clock. Very good dinner—all the neighbors present. Evening adjourned to Mrs. Westalls—danced reels till 10.

14. "Bolivar House," Henry Austin's home on the Brazos River where Mary Austin Holley visited her brother in 1835.

Sunday

E. & H.[165] with Joel & Dr. Jones rode to Bolivar—roads are so bad I declined going.

We took an afternoon ride across the prairie to Leander McNeals—treated with coffee, cakes, champagnes, a liqueur & *kindness*. Live in a cabin in a splendid situation.

12th

Monday
Tremendous rain with thunder & south wind.

Tuesday 13th

Foggy morning—followed by sunshine.
The inhabitants do not remember so long a course of bad weather. Think it is now over.

Wednesday 14th

Came on a norther—very cold, with clouds & light rain—cold increasing.

Thursday 15th

Had a very cold night with ice. The high grass of the prairie is covered with sleet & looks like a vast field of snow—a sad spectacle here. Has not happened since the winter of 1832. They are killing hogs today to salt. They always take a cold time to kill hogs & beef so it will keep. They drive them up & shoot them—having never tasted corn or anything they do not procure themselves, & they are invariably fat—fatter than stall-fed.

Friday 16th

Water froze solid in my room during the night. The prairie was like a sea of glass, glittering in the sunshine. It continued shining & freezing all day. As cold as Boston Commons.

Saturday

The sun rose on the beautiful frost—work of yesterday—like a waving field of silver wheat—which seemed a mimcry rather than anything real. The high verdant oaks were covered with a silver mantle. His brightening beams, however, soon removed the spell with which the Ice King had bound all objects, & trees & animals began to resume their natural appearance & vivacity. The charm dissolved in mist— then came cold rain. It was gloomy in the extreme—for the first time I suffered ennui & homesickness.

I have been too long kept in one place out of the reach of everybody. Have been kept alive by *study*—Spanish & Texas History.

18th

Sunday

The air is mild—& the clouds are breaking away. Hope soon to be revivified by some change in my affairs—The return of brother Henry from his tour of land business will enable me to return. He must have been much exposed during this ferocious weather. Truly the people of Texas dearly earn all they get. Don't care if I never see it again.[166]

Dreamed last night of home—of Harriette—& my husband & of auld lang syne.

19th

Monday

Mild & pleasant. Blessed influence of the sun! With the native Mexican, one is ready to worship it. How natural is such worship! E. & H. came back tonight. Left their father at Bolivar sick. Will soon be down.

20th

Tuesday
A pleasant day & warm.

21st

Wednesday
Cold & rainy. Wrote to William & brother Charles—[167]

Thursday

Pleasant. Went to Quïntana in the wagon—E.—H.—, Mrs. Perry, J. Bryan & myself stopped at Mrs. McKinney's. Met there Mr. St. John & Mr. N. Williams. Ball at Velasco this evening—went over in a skiff after dark. Returned at midnight— Quite a genteel ball. The first opening of the new house which is in the form of an L —being a long room with wings—one for dancing, the other for supper—at which the ladies, 60 in number, were seated. Supper handsome—dressed cakes & sugar pyramids—other confectionary, oranges brought from N Orleans—much order & taste. The rooms new & painted white, have a neat appearance. The ball room was brilliantly lighted by rows of sperm candles over the doors, windows & all round. Mirrors were ranged at each end under which were hair sofas. Round the ceiling were flags festooned displaying the Texas Star, which also waved from the centre cake on the supper table. Had the music of 2 violins mingled with the roar of the sea, upon which you look from the gallery of the house.[168]

23rd

The young ladies returned home after they left Mr. McKenny & the rest determined to attend another ball at the same place this evening. I accompanied them— with Judge & Mrs. Franklin[169] & Miss McConnel. The ball was much the same thing but pleasanter. A piano was in the room, upon which I, very glad to see one, played for the waltzes.[170] Mrs. Wharton[171] invited me to return home with her tomorrow.

24th

Saturday

Having selected my lot in Quintana I went over to the Archer House to join Mrs. Wharton. Took a seat in a barouche & four with Mr. and Mrs. Waller—[172] a beautiful woman—and arrived to dinner. Mr. Wharton & Dr. Jones followed en cheval. The ride must be charming when the roads are dry.

Mr. Wharton is said to have the finest garden in Texas. In it are the remains of a live oak[173] which measures on the ground 64 feet circumference. The largest tree in the world. A cypress at Alixco (Mexico) 76 feet circumference, one at Mitla, Oaxaca (Mexico) 92 feet—some near the city of Mexico—60 feet.

25th

Sunday

After breakfast went into the very pretty garden, much injured by the late frost—

crossed in the boat to the Island, or peninsular, & took the following sketch. This garden is later than usual by a month. The fine figs & orange trees.

26th

Monday

Spend my time delightfully in conversation & books which make the ornaments of the parlor together with various curiosities of nature & art such as shells & fossils —beautiful editions of poetry & philosophy. They have a *stirrup*[174] said to have been worn by Cortez when he conquered Mexico. It is of iron, massive & embossed. Other things in proportion they must have had giant horses. The snuff box of Gen. Castrillon, who fell at Jacinto having on its lid the largest topaz in the world. The box is a horn of the Mexican mountain antelope, its natural curling form lined with gold. The topaz is set in silver. They have a plaster bust of Mr. Preston.

Mr. Wharton lives as *gentlemen* do in other countries with the associations of literature & taste. Is fond of declaiming & reasoning, tastes imbibed, as he says, from his teacher, Mr. Holley, to whose memory he is exceedingly attached. Mrs. Wharton is all that a lady should be—having a cultivated inquiring mind. Converses well.

Mrs. Calvet & her daughter of the neighborhood, with Mrs. Long the widow of the famous Gen. Long came to see us. Several gentlemen visitors were at the house.

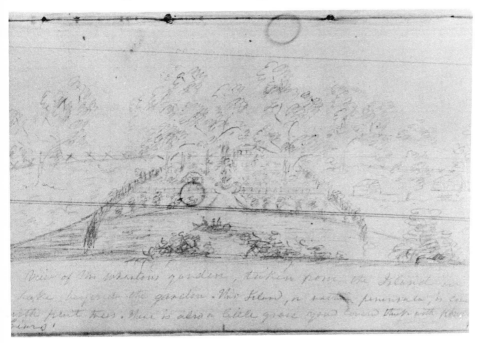

15. "View of Mr. Wharton's garden, taken from the island in a lake beyond the garden. This island, or peninsula, is covered with fruit trees. There is also a little grass yard covered thick with flowery briars."

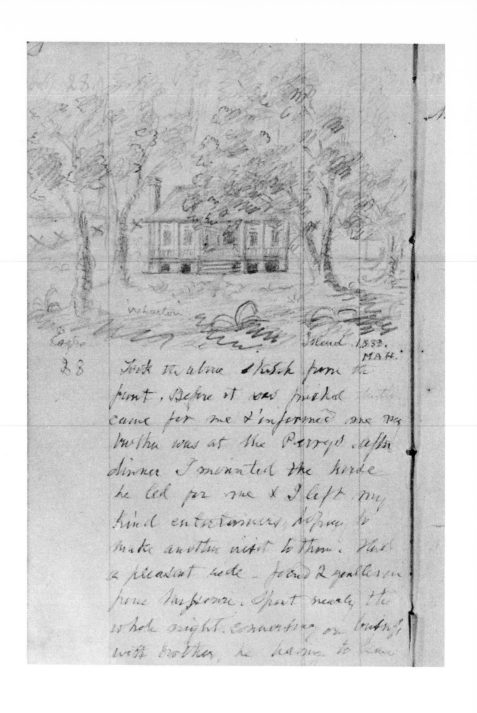

16. "Eagle Island—Wharton's—1837." The house and grounds of Eagle Island plantation were the most splendid of the early Texas plantations.

Tuesday

Dined with Mrs. Calvet & had an agreeable time. Mrs. Long—Drs. Charman—Jones—& Stone[175] a sensible man educated in Cambridge & Boston and Drs. Jackson and Warron, being there. The turkey was delicious—pig—pheasant[?] specially [?]—& other nice things made an excellent dinner. Can see Velasco—6 miles from the place.

28th

Took the above sketch from the point: Before it was finished Austin came for me & informed me my brother was at the Perrys. After dinner I mounted the horse he led for me & I left my kind entertainers, hoping to make another visit to them. Had a pleasant ride—found 2 gentlemen from Missouri. Spent nearly the whole night conversing on business with brother, he having to leave us for Brazoria in the morning.

March 1st

A large company of gentlemen arrived, among them William Scales[176] the purchaser of Quintana Hotel. Mrs. McNeal & Miss Lercette [Lenotte] & Mrs. Blackwell[177] came to dinner & we had a gay day, with plenty of music & talk.

2nd

Thermometer 68—(Mr. Hamilton brought one) drizzling—prevented a proposed ride to Bernard. Miss Lenotte & 2 of the gentlemen staid all night.

Mr. Wharton called his place Eagle Island because on the large tree by the house he found an Eagle seated—a good omen. It is an Island of trees in the prairie.[178]

3rd

68°—10 A.M.—drizzling.

4th

A party of us went to the Bernard, a charming ride on horseback. Found there the oyster men with plenty of oysters—the largest & finest I ever saw. Feasted on them—round a fire of logs & those who preferred had them roasted. With appetite sharpened by the ride & sea air nothing could be more delicious.

One of the gentlemen in the morning with some lucifers set fire to the prairie. There was some wind & it spread rapidly. We had to whip up our horses to fly before it. The hindermost of our party had to pass through the flames. At night it was splendid. A line of fire extended 8 or 9 miles before us. The sun was setting in golden behind us. The sea, with the surf dashing over the beach spread out on the right. A dozen well mounted young persons were pairing off in the distance diverging from our centre—the curlews & the cranes were singing their evening hymn. The wide, wide prairie spreading far & near furnished a scene of surpassing loveliness. One gentleman staid behind with me. We saw the party—2 & 2 enter the line of fire. There were little intervals just to allow a passage. The curling flames rose high making something like an arch over a gateway & shut them from our sight. I said to my companion "this looks very like the entrance to a certain bad place." "True" said he, "but unless we make haste it will be closed before we get there." Sure enough the fire ran faster than our nags. We had to go to another opening farther to the right. We passed. The scene within was imposing. A black carpet covered the surface far ahead & on either side were the lines of flame so that we were completely shut in by fire—whose weird & distant light served to *make the darkness* more *visible*. At length we pass the further line as the first—got out of Hell as we got in—the moon with her attendant planet had then risen & the stars were bright. Never did I witness, in the same scene, so many picturesque objects. What a subject for a painter. To add to its force, at times, I feared, from the confusion of lights, we would be lost. A loud hello from those ahead served to reassure us & tell us the way.[179]

We arrived the last of the party to a late supper.

March 5th

Monday

The fire is still dimly burning—continued till night. Was beautifully brilliant till bed time when the wind changed—it stopped & gradually [went out.? (torn)]

To make excellent bread[180]

Boil 1 lb flour, ¼[?] lb sugar, a small quantity of salt in 2 gallons water for 1 hour. While milk warm bottle & cork it close. It will be fit for use in 24 hours. 1 pint will make 13 lbs. of bread.

11 th June off Velasco North of Brazos. Schooner San Felipe.

March 6th

65°—9 o'clock

Mr. St. John, Mr. N. Williams & Mr. Vernon came to dinner were very merry—came up a thunder gust—had to stay all night.

7th

Went this morning with Mr. Somerville & Mr. Bates[181] to Quintana. Have had the house full completely, full lately—sleep 3 in a bed—Clear & cold (35°) 3 o'clock. E. had a letter from H —

8th

Nothing extraordinary—fine weather. Columbia came—& went without us.

9th

Friday
We all came to the landing to meet the steamboat Crusader[182] for Columbia. The wind blew a gale, & we waited all day for nothing. E. & H. returned to Mrs. Perry's —I staid with Mrs. Crosby.

10th

The girls returned & the boat came & we went on board—Had to stay all night— some agreeable gentlemen[183] were introduced to us, the time passed agreeably.

11th

Sunday
Joel hired a boat & attended by him & Capt. Todd & Mr. Bramen we were rowed 2 miles to Mrs. Sayres.

12th

Monday
Nothing important

13th

Tuesday
Cleared up *finally*—Warm sunshine after a week of clouds & rain. Had a month of fine weather.
We passed a day with Mrs. Nibbs, at the landing, went down in the skiff—pleas-ant. The proprietor of the tavern in Marion pays $1800—good money—a year for

his house—a very ordinary frame building, & $450 per year for cook; $30 per month for a girl. Marion is now called Columbia, being considered a part there of, & is the landing. They propose to connect the two settlements by a rail-road,[184] the present road being miry & inconvenient. The Landing is the most flourishing. It is not very healthy, & last summer, which was a sickly one, more died at Marion, in proportion to the numbers, than elsewhere. Still it is growing fast, & a great deal of business is doing there.

We passed a month with Mrs. Sayre agreeably, but without variety enough to make a record each day. We read, played the piano, & guitar, & back gammon—& conversed a great deal. Rode & walked, & fished in the river. The fish (Buffalo & white cat)[185] were so large as to make it difficult to get them in—Some days we had company, neighbors & from a distance.

I finished reading Zavala's Travels in the U.S.[186] in Spanish—I like the work & mean to get it. I had then my Spanish Telemachus. I also read the astronomical sermons of Chalmers[187] which pleased me. Had never met with it. Do not think his argument conclusive. It is a subject that puzzles me. I found there Latrobe's rambles in Mexico,[188] a small but valuable book, giving details of that country I have not before met with. He was there during Santa Anna's glory, & predicts his down fall much as it happened—that is by the elevation of some other, & rival chieftain—

We hear that he has a considerable force around him at his Hacienda, watching his moment to make a *grito*.[189]

April 1st

At last, Brother having returned, we embarked in the Crusader for Bolivar at 5 in the afternoon. Arrived at supper—the sun setting, & the moon being high in the heavens. It was pleasant, the quiet scenery harmonized well with the moment. We sat out side, not troubled with passengers. One of the few was from near Lexington, he said he had seen me there & that he saw Mr. Warfield in N. Orleans, who informed him there had been no fire in Lexington as we had heard, & nothing extraordinary there—I could not learn his name. The place at Bolivar looks pleasanter than I have ever seen it. The garden is full of roses & peaches, a good fence all round it with multiflora running over it to form a hedge on the bank thrown up by the ditch. The plan is to throw up earth on both sides till it reaches the top of the fence when it will be a bank of roses, where bees may find an inexhaustible source of wealth, & poets, delicious beds.

There is a multiflora that covers an area of 40 to 50 feet. The monthly, or perpetual rose bushes are higher & larger than hogshead.

April 2nd

Thermometer stood at 90°—uncommon for the season.

We set ourselves to work to put things *to rights,* Emily as housekeeper—Henrietta to do little jobs for her father, & I the *out door portion.* I love to work in the open air. I took a hoe, & employed a boy & my self, clearing away rubbish about the yard & garden, making bonfires—planting & transplanting roses found occupation enough to keep off *ennui.*

3rd

Joel Bryan[190] came to see us & passed the night. Mr. Hart, surveyor, arrived to make some changes in the town plot.

Said he had lately been on my league at Dickson's Creek, & that it is a remarkably fine league—that the land is excellent for cultivation: that there is large timber, not only on Dickson, but on a small creek emptying into it, which divides the league nearly in the centre. The timber on this creek is some yards on both sides; that he saw a herd of 30 buffalo[191] there, & great numbers of mustang horses, all perfectly wild.

I asked him what he considered the value of that land. He answered that the person for whom he had been surveying on the adjoining league, all prairie, & not a stick of timber valued his land at $5, & that at that rate mine was worth richly $10. I said I had offered it at $2 & even $1. He said I could at any moment get $2—that Col. — for whom he surveyed, was charmed with my land, & that it was, in fact, a charming place.

The overseer brought in a fine Buck this morning.

7th

Wrote to Horace—took a ride to Oyster Creek, Emily behind me, & Henrietta behind Joel. The ride is charming through the forest—the trees magnificent—meeting nearly at the top, & impervious to the sun. In some places the cane is 30 feet high—took a look at the lake—a lovely spot, nearly round, & surrounded by lofty timber. Will be a glorious residence, no doubt, a hundred years hence. The creek makes the eastern boundary of the Bolivar estate. On the opposite side lives Old Rock, as they call him, & his family. They have cut away the cane & built a house, & enclosure of it. The house is shaped like a tent, in the middle was a fire, over which on a cross piece hung an iron kettle boiling some beef bones, strips of beef undergoing the process of jerking hung on other sticks; a fine looking intelligent boy, like our James, & a laughing, curly-headed, blue-eyed girl, 2½ years old—rosy & fat, were seated round it. They were left in charge of the premises while the father & mother went to Bolivar for corn. On one side, on the ground were the rags which made the bed for the whole family (5 children). This was all the furniture. A red-headed girl of 7, in rags, served as a scare crow in the corn patch—nearby—the young cane disputing ground with its rival the corn—her neck was in blisters & excited my pity, adjoining the house were some turning tools & others—for making chairs &—also covered by canes. The man is a tinker at gun-locks, chairs & springs & wheels. The high cane on every side but the creek served as a barrier to their whole clearing, where neither axe, spade nor hoe had anything to do. I never saw, nor imagined so strange a scene. I can not describe the impression it made on me. What unaccountable poverty. I longed for clothes & food to give the children—& money to place them in better situations. *Jemmy & Betty,* in particular, took strong hold of my sympathy in spite of their rags & dirt.[192]

Returning, full of the subject, we met the old people with the corn on their backs —she, a very wild woman, to appearance slipped off into the woods, retaining, it seems, so much of her sex to be susceptible of shame. He marched on his course & we stopped to talk with him. In his attire he resembled the pictures of Robinson Crusoe, having on a pointed hat of his own manufacture. In his countenance & person he resembled professor Roche & being from dear Ireland, & Roche being the French for Rock, I questioned him about his *kin & country.* He said he was bred within 15 miles of Dublin—that he had some education—that his family spelt their name Roque—but he thought Rock more simple & better, that all 3 of the names prevailed in his country.

He spoke very good English. Is a good surveyor, & excellent mathematician. He has been in Texas 4 years & lived before that in Canada, where he has 2 grown sons. He is ingenious at almost any trade, & has the manners of a man of good condition. The question is, how is it that such a man continues in and is contented with such abject poverty?

1838

April 9th

The moon was eclipsed from before 7 to 9 o'clock. Did not know the meaning of it at first, having no almanac. It commenced below and went off at top, more than half covering the moon as it passed.

14th

This day was distinguished by the arrival to dinner of 3 agreeable young gentlemen. Mr. Smith of N York—living now at Matagorda—Mr. Crook of the house of Crook & Watt—[193] of N York—an Englishman.

18th

Mr. Hatch from Texana came to get some Spanish law, & a deed translated.

Brother absent, I translated the deed for which he paid $4.[194] Had a little shower, the first since we came up.

19th

Cold but no frost.

20th

Overseer killed a fine wild turkey—fat & tender.
Capt. Davis & Mr. Waterhouse came to dinner—from Houston.

21st

Anniversary of the battle of Jacinto[195]—festivals everywhere—heard the report of Canon at Brazoria.

22nd

Sunday has come again & we are not ready—how tedious!
2 steamboats—the Crusader & Laura, are aground a few miles above this place. The first has been there 3 weeks, the latter 1. All well for Bolivar which is the best town site on the river.[196]
The roses & lilacs, (china trees) are in full bloom filling the air with perfume.
It is too dry to plough or work the garden.
It is said that the miasma of unhealthy situations follow the rising sun, therefore have your house on the west side of a Bayou or lake.
The carpenters brought in some vinegar from an oak tree they cut down, of excellent quality. Some gallons can be taken from one tree.[197]

23rd

Mr. Williams of Virginia & 2 others dined here—

25th

6 Carolinians & Georgians (Dr. Lamar, Col. Bonham &c.—passed on from Houston—

29th

A fine shower—the first since we have been here.

Mr. Williams is here—from Quintana—Mr. Patton, near Columbia has planted 300 acres of cotton & 200 acres of corn. The cotton will yield 3 bales, or 1500 lbs clear cotton maise [?]. The corn 40 bush. per acre—corn from 2– to 4 $ per bush.

May 6th

Sunday—Left Bolivar after dinner in the dug-out, or Indian canoe, stopped at Mrs. Sayres, slept at Mrs. Nibbs, Marion.

2nd night at Mrs. Andrews. Mrs. A. gone to N.O. Sent home our own folk & got another smaller dug-out in which we reached Quintana at night. Columbia arrived on the 6th not having touched at Galveston.

8th

Crossed the breakers on a whale boat & in the morning—soon under weigh reached Galveston before dinner. Surprising improvements since I was here 5 months ago.

9th

Waited all day for wood—employed in sketching—went ashore in the boat of the Navy yd. escorted by one of the officers—visited the hotel—Navy yd[198]—all in excellent order—commenced 2 months ago—excellent house for the Commandant. Saw there several Cadets—Mrs. Thompson Wright, Pierce—Miss Hill—visited the Brig of War, Potomac, had refreshments at each.

10th

Started at daylight—further deponent saith[?] not being seasick all the way—but 2 days at sea.

11th

Arrived Saturday night.
Col. Bonham on board.

13th

Arrived in N Orleans.

June 10th

Left N Orleans for home in L. [?] B. Ambassador—in company Mr. & Mrs. Jackes.

17th

Sunday
Arrived in Louisville.

22nd

In Lexington

1838

Books to buy—in N. Orleans: Opinions on various subjects—[199]
dedicated to the Industrious Producer
by William McClure, 1831

Ensayo Historico de las Revoluciones De Mageco desde 1808 hasta 1830
Por Lorenzo de Zavala, Paris 1831 (viage a los Estados Unidos)[200]
Trip to the West & Texas,[201] by A. A. Parker, 1836
Spanish Law Books
Chevalier—travels in U.S.[202]

(fly sheet)
Religion—However we may be disposed to cavil at the idea of natural religion no one can enter the gothic-arched-forests, and the heaven roofed prairies of Texas—the great temple not made with hands, and never profaned by the metaphysics of man—without a profound and elevated devotion.

1. J. P. Bingham Grant, Abstract 4
   on Brazoria–Fort Bend Coun
   Line.

2 and 2a. Highway 288 and Far
   to-Market Road 521 would ha
   been roughly the route Mrs. Holl
   followed from Houston to Br
   zoria.

3. Thomas Alsberry 2 Leagues.

4. J. E. A. Phelps Grant (Orizimb
   Plantation).

5. James E. B. Austin Grant whi
   was developed at the Manor Pla
   tation, Osceola Plantation, a
   Waldeck Plantation.

6. John McNeel Homestead Tract.

7. L. H. McNeel Homestead Tract.

8. J. G. McNeel Homestead Tract.

9. Lowood Plantation, owner Robe
   Mills.

10. Crosby 1000 acre tract.

11. Original Peach Point tract, 19
    acres.

12. Portion of W. Joel Bryan's D
    razno Plantation.

13. Alexander Calvit Grant.

14. West 3½ leagues of the Jared
    Groce 5 League Grant, property
    William H. Wharton and Sara
    Groce Wharton.

15. East 1½ leagues of the 5 Leag
    Grant conveyed to Stephen F. Au
    tin.

16. Approximate location in the Jare
    E. Groce Grant of the Wharto
    Eagle Island home.

17. C. D. Sayre Plantation.

18. Location of Henry Austin's Bol
    var Plantation in the Willia
    Harris Survey.

19. Portion of the William Harris Su
    vey now occupied by The Do
    Chemical Company Reservoir

FIGURES I AND 3. These two sketches show the twin towns of Velasco and Quintana. Although navigation was difficult at the mouth of the Brazos, nevertheless it was the principal port of Austin's colony. Velasco had been platted as a town as early as 1832, and Quintana was probably platted in 1835. Neither Houston nor Galveston existed at this time.

Velasco was one of the first places settled in Austin's colony and was continuously occupied throughout the colonial period. Evidently there was always someone at the mouth of the Brazos to welcome or aid the erring vessels or, more important, to cook the salt which was necessary for the survival of the colonists. Although a great deal of activity took place at the mouth of the Brazos at an early time, there is little information now available about the two towns. We do not know when Velasco was named or for whom. It was designated as one of the places for the establishment of a fort in Texas after the passage of the Law of April, 1830. It would be reasonable to assume that both this designation and its name came from Teran, who was Commander of the Internal Provinces answering directly to the Federal authorities in Mexico City. There were too many prominent persons named Velasco in the history of Mexico to be able to establish the one that Teran may have had in mind. The editor likes to think the town was named for Don Luis de Velasco, 1551–1564, one of the earlier and better Viceroys of Mexico.

Quintana came at a later date than Velasco, principally because it was located on a portion of Stephen F. Austin's premium land. Development of this property began in 1835, but there is no recorded plat of the town of Quintana as originally laid out except for one prepared in 1916 by the owner of the town (principally the heirs of Emily Margaret Perry) which purports to show the original townsite, the river-front tract, and some acreage. However, plats of both Velasco and Quintana were evidently available as early as 1837. (See P. A. Mesier's 1837 Plat, Figure #1A.)

The name of Quintana is as obscure as that of Velasco, but it is likely that the name was selected by Austin to honor Andres Quintana, Under Minister of Foreign Relations of the Mexican Republic in 1822, who contributed as much as any Mexican official toward the final authorization of Austin's original grant. The name of Andres Quintana Roo has also been suggested, as both he and his wife Leona Vicario were prominent in the early period of Mexico's War of Independence, as was her father. To honor the wife, the legislature of Texas and Coahuila in 1827 attempted to change the name of the capital, Saltillo to Leona Vicario (*The Southwestern Historical Quarterly,* Volume XIII, p. 328).

FIGURE 2. Mrs. Holley mentions several times the danger involved in crossing the bar at the entrance to the Brazos. In this sketch, she attempts to give some idea of the location of the wrecked vessels. It is probably the least comprehensive of all her sketches. The following appeared in the *Texas Republican* of Brazoria on May 9, 1835:

"The Schr. Elizabeth was wrecked in attempting to cross the bar at the mouth of the Brazos, on Wednesday last. We have not understood what amount of damage her cargo sustained. We understand she was insured in New Orleans."

FIGURES: 4 and 5 are the only reproductions we have showing the Phelps plantation. Today, none of the original improvements are there and the property is not owned by the heirs. Though Mrs. Holley has previously referred to the beautiful arbor of trees leading from the house to the river, here she says the house is on the prairie. Figure 5 is from a painting of a later date.

FIGURE 6 evidently represents the living quarters of the family that Mrs. Holley describes as "the family of Old Rock" in the diary, April 7, 1838. Mrs. Holley has no information under this sketch.

FIGURE 7. Mrs. Holley's sketch is our only source of information about improvements made on the Sayre plantation. The house was destroyed and its owner evidently gone from Brazoria County at an early date. No information after the early 1850s has been found about the Sayres or their home. Charles D. Sayre acquired his two-thousand-acre plantation site on the east side of the Brazos in 1832 by deeds from James Brit Bailey and disposed of it in 1856.

The original sketch reads in full: "Plantation of Mr. Sayre on the Brazos, 40 miles from the sea. ½ league. This house, 56 by 40, cost from $800 to 1000. Cotton gin $1000. 100 bales cotton this year—1200 bushels corn-potatoes [in] second year of cultivation— 100 acres in cotton. Refused $1500 for land. Purchased by him [Sayre] for $500.00."

FIGURES 8, 9, 10A, 10B, AND 11 are all of Houston or its environs.

FIGURE 8. I think we are safe in assuming that this sketch is the earliest facsimile of the old Capitol and was done at the time that it was actually being used. As noted below (Note #81), Mrs. Holley gives a rather dismal description of Houston's quarters, a reaction shared by other visitors of the time. It is odd that with all the buildings in Houston at this time, the President had not secured better quarters.

The Allen home was located on Lot 6, Block 48, next door to Houston's quarters, at the northwest corner of Prairie & Caroline Street. (See Note #79) Mrs. Holley was evidently a visitor in the Augustus Allen home at the time this sketch was made. There is no information available to date regarding the American Ministry, which is in front of the Capitol, nor has it been possible to obtain any information regarding the three small buildings to the rear.

FIGURE 9 shows, among other things, a house which evidently belonged to Felix Huston in 1837, and was located on Lot #1, Block 45—the northwest corner of Prairie Avenue and Fannin Street. Huston was one of many hotheads that the State of Mississippi was able to contribute to Texas. He was an agitator, duelist, and an extremely ambitious man. His great notoriety in Texas may have resulted from the fact that he failed to kill Albert Sidney Johnston in their famous duel shortly after San Jacinto. Huston's residence in Texas was short lived, as he returned to Mississippi in 1837. (See M. K. Wisehart's *Sam Houston: American Giant*, page 304.) Mrs. Holley says the first house was built January 1836, but information based on the research of Andrew Forest Muir indicates that it was January 1837. (See *Texas in 1837*. Austin: University of Texas Press, p. 189.)

FIGURE 10A. (See reference to Barnard E. Bee in Note #88.) This rather inconspicuous little house, with the kitchen or servant quarters in the back, is probably typical of most of the houses in Texas at this time. It is the editor's belief that Eagle Island was the only manorial plantation home built in Texas during the colonial period, and that the other showplaces such as Ellersly, Liendo, and the Patton-Varner plantations came at a considerably later date.

FIGURE 10B. There is presently no information available regarding Mrs. Milon or her boarding house.

FIGURE 11. This appears to be a view of one of Houston's saloons. A. Pat Daniel's, *Texas Ave. at Main,* mentions that several "groceries" were housed in semi-permanent tents. Kesler's famous saloon was located between Franklin & Congress Avenues.

The several tents that were pitched in Houston at this time were famous more for liquor sales than other commodities.

FIGURES 12 and 13, Peach Point, show the home that James F. Perry built on a tract acquired from Stephen F. Austin in the early 1830s. (See Note 49 on James F. and Emily Margaret Perry.) Mrs. Holley made another sketch of Peach Point, now preserved in the archives at the University of Texas. Figure 13 is from a ferrotype of a later date.

The record seems clear that the house was built in 1832, and Stephen F. Austin was insistent that his brother-in-law get to work on a new home where he would have quarters. Austin had drawn plans for the house and had made definite suggestions about its construction, but evidently his plans were not followed (see Austin's House Plans, *The Austin Papers*, Vol. II, pp. 715–20). There is still preserved at Peach Point a portion of the house, the left front (actually two rooms in all), which was Austin's study and bedroom. There are dioramas of Peach Point in the San Jacinto Museum and in the Texas Memorial Museum in Austin. The house remained in fairly good repair until the 1915 hurricane when irreparable damage was done. Since that time, the Perry family has maintained only the two rooms mentioned above. As the Peach Point property began to dwindle through sale, partition, and disastrous conditions following the Civil War, the homestead tract of two hundred acres was set aside. This property has passed from James F. Perry to his son, S. S. Perry; from S. S. Perry to his son, James F. Perry; and James F. Perry willed the property to his widow, Catherine Norris Perry. She partitioned the property in three tracts, leaving one to her daughter, Cassie Perry Bryan, who is still living at Peach Point where she was born, a second to her son, S. S. Perry, who willed his interest to his son, S. S. Perry, Jr., who now resides on the place, and to his daughter, Mrs. P. R. Hamill, who resides in Bay City, and the third to her granddaughter, Mrs. John Ward Berretta (nee Mary Austin Perry) of San Antonio, Texas. The Perry heirs live in other houses on the tract; but they have preserved, in excellent condition, the two rooms of the original house—and Mrs. Hamill has restored many of the pictures and furniture and a number of Austin's personal possessions. The heirs, in recent years, have re-acquired a substantial portion of the original Peach Point tract. A number of heirs of Henry Austin Perry, the brother of the second James F. Perry, reside in close proximity to the Peach Point homestead tract and on a portion of the original holdings.

FIGURE 14. Mrs. Holley's brother Henry's house, where she stayed during most of her 1835 visit, was built in the early 1830s on land acquired in the William-Harris League.

Probably never a very pretentious place, the house had been destroyed even before the time of Abner J. Strobel, chronicler of Brazoria County plantations, in the early 1870s. In addition to clearing a portion of the property for cultivation, Henry Austin operated a ferry and had a tavern of sorts. The property was located at the head of tidewater on the Brazos, a tidal stream in which fresh water flows above the salt water for some distance.

Mrs. Holley's sketch reads: "Bolivar House, Texas. This plantation, 1700 acres—worth $50.00 per acre, and that of Mr. Sayre are 2 of the best on the Brazos. 2000 lbs. cotton per acre are a common crop in Texas. 2500 to 3000 have been raised."

Note also the inscription at the top of the sketch, "Mary A. Dall from Mother—Nov. 1886." The mother referred to is Harriette Brand, Mrs. Holley's daughter.

FIGURES 15 AND 16. The gardens and house of the Eagle Island plantation were famous, as befitted the home of the Wharton and Groce families who occupy an important place in Texas history. Though a great deal has been written about these families, there is little information about them at this early period. The personal lives of William H. Wharton, John A. Wharton, and Jared E. Groce are rather obscure when compared to such of their contemporaries as Austin, Houston, Lamar, Anson Jones, Henry Smith, and other prominent settlers along the lower Brazos River—principally due to the early demise of all three. We are familiar with the public affairs of the well-known brothers (see Note #131), as well as the wealthy planter, but little of their correspondence and few adequate character sketches have been preserved. In a funeral eulogy John Wharton was called "the keenest blade at San Jacinto," but his principal act of heroism while on the battlefield seems to have been an attempt to prevent the Texans from killing Mexicans who had already surrendered.

Jared E. Groce was by far the richest man who came to Texas and he brought a great deal of equipment for agricultural development and at least eighty slaves. (Deed records show Austin's recommendation that he be given two haciendas, or ten leagues.)

His daughter, Sarah A. Groce, married William H. Wharton in 1827 and their Eagle Island home was the first frame house built in Austin's colony, the lumber having been imported from another state. At this time, William was just beginning practice as a young lawyer in a new land. During his life Eagle Island was certainly the most elegant place in Austin's colony. The gardener came from either Scotland or Belgium, and the grounds must have encompassed at least twenty acres.

Mrs. Holley writes more on the contents of the house and of the garden than of the house itself. Her sketch shows a smaller house than the one reproduced here from an early water color in possession of a member of the Wharton family. (See page 125.) It may have been that there were additions to the house at a later date, which was the case in many early Brazoria County plantations. Actually, it was during the period from the sugar cultivation of the early 1840s until the Civil War that the people along the Brazos River acquired the funds to build the fabulous places like Ellersly (the Greenville McNeel plantation) and the sugar mills. (See Ellersly, page 128 and the Waldeck plantation sugar mill).

The Eagle Island plantation homesite is now partially owned by the Restwood Memorial Park Cemetery Association, and on the property are State markers purporting to locate the graves of William H. Wharton, John A. Wharton, and Branch T. Archer. Likewise, there are tombs, probably placed by the family, showing the grave sites of Sarah A. Wharton, Mrs. Penelope Wharton (wife of the Confederate general), and their child, Katherine Wharton.

Eagle Island plantation originally contained approximately 16,000 acres. It was also at one time the site of a part of three other famous plantations: the Lake Jackson plantation, Retrieve plantation, and the Evergreen plantation. The plantation covered perhaps the finest tract of land in Brazoria County, bordering Oyster Creek throughout its whole length. By the time of the death of Sarah A. Wharton in 1879, most of the estate had been disposed of; and when William Wharton Groce sold the two-hundred-acre home tract in the early part of the twentieth century, all of the Groce and Wharton interest in the land passed.

The south 1½ leagues were acquired by Stephen F. Austin from Jared E. Groce and eventually passed to his nephew, Moses Austin Bryan, a substantial portion (known as Stratton Ridge) being still owned by some of the Bryan heirs (Fred A. Brock, J. T. S. Brock, and Mrs. Lois Brock Adriance).

NOTES

1. When Mrs. Holley boarded the *San Felipe* at New Orleans, she could not know what an important part the ship was to play in the early history of Texas. On September 1, 1835, the little vessel, now commanded by Captain William A. Hurd and armed for combat, arrived off Velasco bearing as its most important passenger the empresario Stephen F. Austin, who had been recently released from prison in Mexico City and was returning to Texas via New Orleans. The *San Felipe* had been purchased in New Orleans by Thomas F. McKinney at a price of $8,965, including freight on board "when taken." The Mexican warship *Correo,* commanded by Captain T. M. Thompson, an Englishman in the service of the Mexican Government, had already captured a Texas vessel, the *Tremont,* when the *San Felipe* arrived at Velasco. Austin was landed at Velasco, and the *San Felipe* went off to join the conflict and succeeded in capturing the *Correo,* which was later taken to New Orleans as a prize.

REFERENCES:

Jim Dan Hill, *The Texas Navy* (Chicago: University of Chicago Press, 1937), pp. 25–31.
Dr. Alex Dienst, *The Navy of the Republic of Texas* (limited edition of 20 volumes, privately printed, 1909), pp. 2–6.
David B. Edward, *The History of Texas* (Cincinnati: J. A. James & Company), p. 249.
Eugene C. Barker, *The Life of Stephen F. Austin, Founder of Texas, 1793–1836* (Austin: Texas State Historical Association, 1949), p. 410.

2. It seems strange that a person who was born in Connecticut and had spent a good part of her life in Boston would refer to anyone as a "good Yankee lady." It would be appropriate to think that Mrs. Holley was referring to a woman of industry, integrity, and stability.

It was at the home of John Haskells in Boston that the Holleys boarded for several years.

REFERENCES:

Rebecca Smith Lee, *Mary Austin Holley, A Biography* (Austin: University of Texas Press, 1962), pp. 81, 101, 102, 111.

3. Seasickness was certainly a problem for Mrs. Holley, but it did not seem to deter her travel.

4. It is impossible to establish definitely the identity of many persons whose names appear in this diary. We know that there was a William Hawley in Texas in 1835, a Timothy Treadwell and a Daniel Treadwell, a James Turnbull and an R. Turnbull: but there is no way of locating these people along the Brazos at the time Mrs. Holley was there, and none gained enough prominence to have attracted historians of that period.

General Edmund Pendleton Gaines is credited with having helped the Texas cause during the Revolution by moving a detachment of U. S. Army troops from Fort Jessup, Louisiana, to Nacogdoches upon the invitation of Stephen F. Austin. Mrs. Holley's acquaintance with General Gaines evidently extends over a period of time, as she saw him in New Orleans several years later.

REFERENCES:

Lee, *op. cit.,* pp. 358–59.
Allen Johnson, Dumas Malone (ed.), *Dictionary of American Biography* (New York: Charles Scribner's Sons, 1958), IV, p. 192.

5. This Mrs. Nibbs appears to be the wife of Willis Nibbs, who, for a short period in 1835,

was the law partner of William B. Travis in San Felipe, Texas (*The Texas Republican,* San Felipe, February 14, 1836).

6. This is the story of the bar at the Brazos River which worried the colonists and many others for years. It was not until the early 1930s, when the flow of the river was diverted to a new channel that a permanent harbor was established at the mouth of the Brazos River. (See Sketch #2 for reference to the vessel *Elizabeth*.)

REFERENCES:

Early Minutes of Brazos River Harbor Navigation District.

7. Benjamin Fort Smith was born January 2, 1796, in Logan County, Kentucky. Before he was nineteen years old, he was promoted to major while a member of the staff of Andrew Jackson at the Battle of New Orleans. He came to Texas in 1832 and became a resident citizen of Austin's colony in 1833. He acquired land on Oyster Creek and the lower Brazos and was deeply involved in the illegal slave trade. During the Revolution, Smith commanded a company at Gonzales and later fought in Karnes' company at San Jacinto. Smith represented Montgomery County in the Fifth Congress in 1841 and died at Sulphur Springs in 1841. He never married and was much in the company of his sister, Sarah D. Terry, widow of Joseph R .Terry. His mother, Obedience Smith, was one of the early settlers of Houston; and her home has been restored by the Harris County Heritage Society.

8. McKinney was previously referred to as the purchaser of the *San Felipe* (Note #1). He was a business partner with Samuel May Williams in Williams and McKinney, a firm formed in 1834, and these two played an important part in the financial history of the colonial period, the Republic, and the State of Texas. The business was started in Brazoria but was transferred to Quintana within the year. On December 25, 1835, Stephen F. Austin wrote to James F. Perry, his brother-in-law, from Quintana:

"I have had a conversation with McKinney about laying off a town at this place—After Williams returns, you and McKinney and he can consult on the subject and lay out the lots here, have a handsome map made of them, and sell them to the best advantage without waiting for my return. . . . To avoid all difficulty or misunderstanding in case of my death, I will now say to you that I intend to make a present to McKinney and Williams—of the lot where their warehouse is." (*The Austin Papers,* ed. by Eugene C. Barker, III, 294–95.)

A great deal has been written about Samuel May Williams, and his papers have been preserved and edited. It is a shame that there is not a comprehensive biography of McKinney because he was certainly one of the most powerful and influential of early Texans. A good but perhaps prejudiced description of his relationship with Stephen F. Austin is reflected by the letter from Moses Austin Bryan to his son Beauregard Bryan, dated September 25, 1889:

"He took back his confidence from both Williams and McKinney, and they knew it, for he was plain in defining his position; that they had been untrue to Texas, and to him when he was in prison by turning "land jobbers." I was at Peach Point with Austin after he became a candidate for President. He was laying on a cot in the gallery and saw McKinney coming up the walk in the yard. Austin received him so coldly that McKinney immediately left and got up the meeting in Columbia that nominated Houston. Williams and McKinney were largely interested in the four hundred league grant, which was made by the State at Montclova to Williams and his associates. McKinney wanted Austin to endorse it which he positively refused to do. McKinney had for many years been the warm personal friend of Austin, and they were warmly attached to each other. McKinney was no ordinary man, bold and outspoken, generous, warm-hearted, enthusiastic and devoted to his friends and a bitter enemy—of strong partialities and prejudices, he could see no faults in friends and no virtues in enemies. He wanted his friends to be to him what he was willing to be to them, and broke with them when he relied on them and they did not sustain him, without reference to right or wrong. It was thus with him in reference to Austin in the election . . ." (The Beauregard Bryan Papers, (The Archives), University of Texas Library).

McKinney was also the subject of a colorful comment in the *Journal of Francis Sheridan, 1839–1840,* Sheridan being a young, cynical, and at times, witty Irishman, on a visit to Texas as a minor official in the British Diplomatic Service. Sheridan is leaving Velasco on the *Constitution* for Galveston Island:

". . . However, we at last got on & I had an opportunity of looking at my fellow passengers. The first that struck me was a gentleman apparently of about 40 years, attired in a frock coat made out of a scarlet blanket with a black edging, and picking his teeth with a Bowie Knife. In this unpretending employment was engaged no less a personage than Mr. McKinnie of the firm of McKinnie & Williams, the Barings of Texas. On further acquaintance, I found him to be far superior to the general run of Texians and acknowledged by all to be a very honest, charitable & wirthy man. He has been the making of Galveston. Among other eccentricities of the remarkable man was one which I much admired. He never had any fixed hours for grubbins—always eating when he was hungry & drinking when dry. His Partner followed him strictly in the latter—but then he was always dry. The only other person of note on board was a red-headed gentleman in a tanned deerskin doublet, &—liquor. This garment, however, he doffed on the following day & appeared in a green blanket frock & black border, jealous I suppose, of the gawdy McKinnie." (*Galveston Island, The Journal of Francis Sheridan, 1839–1840,* edited by Willis W. Pratt, University of Texas Press, Austin, Texas, 1954.)

REFERENCES:

Johnson, Malone, *op. cit.,* X, pp. 289–90.
Ruth G. Nichols, *Samuel May Williams, 1795–1858* (Galveston: Rosenberg Library Press, 1956).
Ruth G. Nichols, S. W. Lifflander, *Calendar to Samuel May Williams Papers,* p. xiv (Rosenberg).
Amelia W. Williams, Eugene C. Barker (ed.) *Writings of Sam Houston* (Austin: University of Texas Press, 1938), IV, pp. 34–36.

9. There must have been a real distinction in Mrs. Holley's mind between men and gentlemen.

The Perry-Bryan Papers, (the Archives), the University of Texas Library.

10. It is unfortunate that Mrs. Holley does not give any further identification of Mr. Patton. There were several Patton brothers in Texas at this time and at least two were prominent.

At an early date, Columbus R. Patton purchased the Varner League, originally granted in 1824 to Martin Varner, and developed one of the finest plantations on the Brazos. The property was eventually acquired by Governor James S. Hogg and passed to his heirs who maintained and restored most of the early improvements on the property. A portion of the property, which included the principal improvements, was given to the State of Texas by Miss Ima Hogg of Houston, Texas. There has probably been no finer job of restoration and redecoration of an early Texas plantation home than the work of the Hogg heirs on the Varner-Patton improvements. It might be worth mentioning also that the Varner League made up a part of what is known as the West Columbia oil field which was discovered in 1920. This is one of the salt dome oil fields in Texas which has produced more than 100,000,000 barrels of oil.

William H. Patton was a brother of Columbus Patton. He came to the area now known as Brazoria County at an early date and was active in the affairs of Texas during the colonial and revolutionary periods. He was at the Battle of Velasco in 1832 and at the

Siege of Bexar, and was one of Sam Houston's aides-de-camp at San Jacinto. W. H. Patton was one of the group selected to accompany Santa Anna to the United States, and Mrs. Holley would have had an opportunity to renew her acquaintance when she met the party at Louisville, Kentucky, and interviewed Santa Anna.

REFERENCES:

J. P. Bryan, Research on Brazoria County (notes on Battle of Velasco).
Alice Kilman, unpublished research.
Lee, *op. cit.,* p. 280.

11. Neither the Mr. Stephenson referred to, nor Mr. Berryman was particularly prominent in local affairs at the time of the killing, and little information is available about either. Evidently James Berryman was associated with Anson Jones in the practice of medicine at this time in Brazoria. On February 14, 1837, there was a probate proceeding on the estate of James M. Berryman, which is Cause #70 of the probate records of Brazoria County. Dr. Anson Jones made the application and listed as the only asset a certificate for a headright of land. Jones, while himself ill in Brazoria, wrote:

"During my sickness, my business was attended to by Dr. Berryman, a gentleman who had just completed his medical studies in my office, and who was, not long after, killed in a duel with R. A. Stevenson." (Pat Ireland Nixon, *History of Medicine in Texas,* Lancaster, Pennsylvania: Lancaster Press, 1946, p. 317.)

All that is known about Mr. Stephenson is the following advertisement:
"Mr. M. W. Smith having purchased Mrs. Jane Long's Public House [it is] to be run by Mr. and Mrs. Stephenson." (*The Advocate of the Peoples Rights,* Brazoria, Texas, February 22, 1834.)

Regardless of the importance of the participants, muskets at ten paces would certainly be an effective method of dueling.

12. Mrs. Holley was extremely conscious of the weather in Texas and in all her writings she gives detailed accounts. Most of the time she makes it really good and unusual, but like everyone else, she finally discovers that it is almost impossible to cope with these unpredictable phenomena.

13. It is odd that Mrs. Holley did not mention the steamboat *Ariel* that her brother Henry had operated on the Rio Grande and brought with him to Brazoria in the summer of 1830. There is no evidence that Henry Austin attempted to operate the boat on the Brazos, and it was eventually wrecked on the San Jacinto River near the present city of Houston. The first steamboat on the Brazos was either the *Cayuga* or the *Yellowstone.*

REFERENCES:

William Ransom Hogan, *Life and Letters of Henry Austin, 1782–1852,* pp. 214–16.
The Texas & Telegraph Register, Brazoria, Texas, March 2, 1837.

14. Mrs. Holley entered the mouth of the Brazos on October 22, 1831, on board the ship *Spica.* The following was her first impression:
"On our right, in front of their palmetto-roofed, and windowless barracks, the lazy sentinels were 'walking their lonely rounds,' without excessive martial parade; nor did the unturretted quarters of the commanding officer show forth much of the blazonry of a Spanish Don. There was no tree, no cultivation. A uniform verdure alone, indicated the reason of the year. Nothing marked civilization, save a fabric for making salt; itself an image of desolation, and the solitary house of the pilot, standing high on piles, serving, at once, for a beacon for the mariner, and a refuge from the storm. The whole appearance of the scene at the north with the associ-

ations of a northern climate, would be called bleak; but in this latitude, the dark blue sea, when not made terrific by a storm, always suggests agreeable images to the mind, especially that of a refreshing coolness." (Mary Austin Holley, *Texas: Observations, Historical, Graphical, and Descriptive, in a Series of Letters Written During a Visit to Austin's Colony with a View to a Permanent Settlement in that County in the Autumn of 1831;* Baltimore: Armstrong & Plaskitt, 1833), p. 24.

15. The Mexican soldiers had been expelled after the Battle of Velasco, a preliminary of the Texas Revolution, in June of 1832, and there is no indication that the fort was ever manned again. Evidently the customs collector at this time was operating in Brazoria. The actual beginning of Velasco as a town and the origin of its name are obscure, but it is assumed that is was named and designated as a port of entry soon after the passage of the Law of 1830. (See further information about Velasco, Sketches # 1 & 3.)

REFERENCES:

Eugene C. Barker, "Establishment of Custom Houses," *Southwestern Historical Quarterly,*
    XIII, pp. 259–60.
John Henry Brown, *History of Texas,* I, pp. 182–88 (the Battle of Velasco).

16. We assume that Mr. White is Walter C. White, who was one of Austin's Old Three Hundred, and conducted a mercantile business with James Knight at San Felipe de Austin and other places along the Brazos.

17. At this time Henry Austin, whose home was at Bolivar on the Brazos, had two girls and three boys. Their names were: Henrietta, Emily, Edward Trailer, James, and Henry.

REFERENCES:

William Ransom Hogan, *op. cit.,* p. 27.

18. The rivalry between Brazoria and Columbia was a continuing one during the colonial period; the seat of government was moved back and forth between Columbia and Brazoria at least three times.
"In 1832 the Congress of the State of Coahuila and Texas created the Municipality of Brazoria with the town of Brazoria its seat of Justice, and John Austin became the first Alcalde at Brazoria. Henry Smith was Alcalde of Municipality of Brazoria in 1833 and Edwin Waller in 1834. Papers signed by John Austin, Alcalde in 1832, by Henry Smith, Alcalde in 1833, and Edwin Waller, Alcalde in 1834, are in the courthouse, as is the docket of Edwin Waller for part of the year 1834. The Alcalde was a higher officer than the comisario and had general judiciary authority as well as administrative authority.
"The location of the seat of justice of the Municipality of Brazoria soon became an issue. In April of 1834 the Congress of the State of Coahuila and Texas passed a decree removing the seat of justice from Brazoria to Columbia (the town now known as West Columbia) and changing the name of the municipality from Brazoria to Columbia. This decree was apparently passed in pursuance of an election held in the municipality and a petition of citizens of the municipality to Congress. Besides stating that the election had resulted in favor of Columbia, the reason given for the change was that petitioners were assured that Columbia was the "most suitable of the two for the accommodation of the citizens who may have business with the authorities of the Jurisdiction as it is situated on dry ground, on the edge of a large prairie, which spreads itself out for the accommodation of cattle and horses, of which a good number is always necessary to transient visitors, whereas the town of Brazoria is placed deep in a timbered bottom and in wet seasons almost inaccessible. Among the signers of the petition were J. H. Bell, Warren D. C. Hall, George Tennille, W. H. Patton, Thos. Davis, John D. Patton, Wm. T. Austin, Jas. Ray Phillips, M. C. Patton, Thos F. McKinney, Columbus R. Patton, Joseph M. McCormick, Sidney Phillips, George S. Penticost, David McCormick and others. [Note the Patton signers.]

"The change of the seat of justice from Brazoria to Columbia proved unsatisfactory as it appears that as soon as February 22, 1835, an election was held to remove the seat of justice back to Brazoria. This election evidently failed to carry as Columbia remained the seat of justice until the General Consultation of Texas, which met at San Felipe de Austin on October 16, 1835, passed a resolution on November 12, 1835, removing the seat of justice from Columbia back to Brazoria and changing the name of the Municipality from Columbia back to Brazoria. This did not settle the question, and on October 31, 1837, the Congress of the Republic of Texas, by joint resolution, authorized an election to be held on November 20, 1837, to determine whether the seat of justice should remain at Brazoria or be removed to Columbia. This election failed to carry and on December 14, 1837, the Congress of the Republic of Texas passed a joint resolution declaring Brazoria to be the permanent seat of justice of Brazoria County." (*The County Seat Issue for Texas Centennial 1936* by Louis J. Wilson.)

REFERENCES:

The Historical Records Survey, 1937, No. 3 Municipality of Brazoria (Inventory of the Colonial Archives of Texas, 1821–1837).

19. Evidently the cholera epidemic of 1833 took a greater toll of lives in Brazoria than any other part of the colony. In October 1833, James F. Perry wrote to Stephen F. Austin:
"there has been recently a good deal of sickness at San felepe and above and a good many deaths in our neighborhood we have lost old Mr. McNeel (fever) Mr. Westall, James and Emeline (cholera) and Mr. Munson (fever) which leves a very considerable vackancey here in Brazoria our friend john austin both his children Mrs. Wm austin—Anthony the printer, Bradly and a number of negroes all died at Westall with the cholara, there was six or seven corps there at one time before they could be buried as the neighbours were afraid to approach them a great many more of your acquantances you will find gon among them are Doctr Cox and counsel. counsels wife and child. Jno Cox on the Bernard and a number of others not recolected it is said there was 80 persons died at Brazoria in the course of the summer and Velasco was nearly depopulated by the cholera." (*The Austin Papers*, 1922, Vol. II, page 1010.)

REFERENCES:

J. Villasana Haggard, "Epidemic Cholera," *Southwestern Historical Quarterly*, XL, p. 216.

20. The Andrews evidently ran a boarding house in Brazoria for some time as Mrs. Holley stayed with them again in 1838. Edmund Andrews, while not necessarily one of the most prominent citizens of Brazoria, was active in the affairs of the colony and Republic. There are a good many real-estate and probate transactions in which he was interested as reflected by the early records of Brazoria County. Of more than passing interest is the following note which appears in the probate papers of the estate of James W. Fannin, Jr., No. 162, from 1826 to 1843:
"Mr Edmund Andrews
                    or
Robert Mills & Co.

My friend Capt. Bullock is too unwell with measles to go by water—and proceeds by land to Copen—He has spent several hundred dollars in bringing to our aid his company —and is now with out resources
I am nearly so—and must ask you or either of you to advance him from twenty to fifty dollars and I will repay it when I get back—and greatly oblige

yr friend &c etc.
J. W. Fannin Jr"

Robert Mills, the other addressee, was a prominent planter and merchant in Brazoria County and was supposed to have been the wealthiest man in Texas prior to the Civil War.

REFERENCES:

Brazoria Historical Records Survey.

21. John Austin's widow, Elizabeth E. Austin, married Dr. T. F. L. Parrott in 1834. She later sold a portion of the 2-League Grant on Buffalo Bayou to the Allen brothers, who began the development of the city of Houston.

John Austin, who played an important part in the early history of Texas, was not an Austin relative but a business associate of Stephen F. Austin's younger brother, James E. B. Austin. He was born in New Haven, Connecticut, and the *Handbook of Texas* lists the date of his birth as 1801. This date would make him considerably younger than Stephen F. Austin, whereas the editor's general impression is that he was older. His father, for whom he was named John Punderson Austin, was a graduate of Yale and a minister. John Austin left home at an early age and after many adventures in foreign countries appears on the Texas scene as one of James Long's lieutenants. In 1822, John Austin and Ben Milam went to Mexico City to intercede in behalf of James Long, who was being held prisoner there. John Austin evidently met Stephen F. Austin in Mexico City at this time and joined his colony at an early date.

In 1828, on land belonging to Stephen F. Austin, or rather out of the Stephen F. Austin 7 1/3-League Grant, John Austin laid out the town of Brazoria.

From the unpublished papers of Louis J. Wilson prepared in 1936, and in possession of J. P. Bryan:

"Listed in the inventory of the Estate of John Austin, who died in 1833, is 'Brick Store on Lot No. 1, Block 13,' in Brazoria, appraised at $1,050.00, also listed '2 leagues of land on Buffalo Bayou,' appraised at $3,600.00.

"When I first noticed these items in the inventory of John Austin's estate some thirty years or more ago, I made inquiry about the little brick building then and still on Lot 1, in the Block No. 13, in Brazoria; and I am satisfied that it is the lower story of the building listed in the inventory of John Austin's estate and was, therefore, constructed by John Austin prior to his death in 1833. It is now used as part of the Williamson store, the only business house remaining in the old town of Brazoria; and except for such use it is now almost without value.

"The original town of Houston was laid off on part of John Austin's two leagues of land on Buffalo Bayou and the two leagues are now covered by Houston and are worth millions."

John Austin was a leader in the so-called disturbances at Anahuac and was the commander of the Texan forces at the Battle of Velasco in June of 1832. He died in the cholera epidemic of 1833 and is buried on what is known as the Westall place in Brazoria County.

REFERENCES:

Brazoria Historical Records Survey, (marriage contract of T. F. L. Parrott and Elizabeth E.
    Austin) #13, p. 25.
Holley, *op. cit.*, pp. 248–50 (short biography of John Austin Estate).
A. F. Muir, Research Notes.
Records of Brazoria County: Probate Proceedings of John Austin Estate, Cause No. 14.

22. William T. Austin's wife did die in the cholera epidemic, and he married again within a short time. He maintained his brother's loyalty to Stephen F. Austin and even fought a duel with John Wharton because of the things he said about either Stephen F. Austin or William's brother John.

William T. Austin was prominent in the public affairs of Texas from the colonial period until it became a state. The election-return records of Brazoria County indicate that he served as county clerk for some time but resigned on December 22, 1838. He was Stephen F. Austin's aide-de-camp at the Siege of Bexar and, likewise, one of Sam Houston's aides-de-camp. When Houston's army reached the Brazos, William T. Austin was dispatched to Velasco to make some effort to fortify this important port.

REFERENCES:

J. P. Bryan, *op. cit.,* II, p. 235.
Robert E. Davis (ed.), "E. M. Pease Letters, 1836–1841," *Texana,* Vol. II, No. 4, p. 309.

23. "His aged father" was John Punderson Austin, Sr., who had come to visit John Austin, having learned that his son was favorably established in a colony; and he also died of cholera soon after his arrival.

REFERENCES:
Mary Austin Holley, *loc. cit.*

24. Marion and Bell's Landing and East and West Columbia have been names that have caused a good bit of confusion for historians. Marion, or Bell's Landing, was the port of Columbia—if it could be called that. This area is now called East Columbia, and the location of Columbia, first capital of Texas, is now West Columbia, an incorporated town. (Early plats of both East and West Columbia are recorded in Brazoria County Records, Plat Book No. 4.)

East Columbia today is an historical showplace for those interested in the preservation of the old colonial homes. There are in existence, and in a wonderful state of repair, six homes, all over one hundred years of age; the oldest being 125 years old. Four of the homes are occupied by the descendants of the original builders.

REFERENCES:

Mary Nixon Rogers, "History of Brazoria County" (article about Columbia houses published by Brazoria County Federation of Women's Clubs, 1940).
Mrs. M. M. Galloway, telephone conversation with J. P. Bryan, December 1964.

25. Bell referred to is Josiah Hughes Bell, who was a close friend of Austin, and who was left in charge of the affairs of the colony when Austin went to Mexico City to obtain approval of his grant. He served as Alcalde at Washington-on-the-Brazos, evidently in 1822, and is often referred to by historians as the "old Alcalde."

The towns of East and West Columbia are on the Josiah H. Bell League (Abstract #40) in Brazoria County.

REFERENCES:

Eugene C. Barker (ed.), *The Austin Papers, 1919* (Washington: Government Printing Office, 1924–1928), II, p. 533.

26. Henry Austin was the second son of Elijah and Esther Austin and was Mrs. Holley's favorite brother. Forced to make his own living at an early age because of the death of his father, Henry traveled widely and engaged in various businesses over a good part of the world. He evidently engaged in some successful ventures but most seemed short lived. In the 1820s he became interested in Mexico and built a steamboat, which he named the *Ariel,* to develop commerce on the Rio Grande River. Henry said that he roomed with Robert Fulton in New York. Failing to find enough business to justify this operation, he came to Austin's colony in 1830 with his boat. (See reference to the *Ariel* in Texas in Note 13.) From the beginning of his stay in the colony, Henry Austin was a land speculator. His previous activities on the Rio Grande qualified him as one who would receive, under the laws of Texas and Coahuila, an eleven-league grant of land. His application for the grant was approved by the government, and he located his tracts throughout what was

then known as the Counties of Brazoria, Washington, Fayette, and Colorado. His head-quarters were on a tract of land at the head of tidewater on the Brazos, forty-five miles from the river's mouth by water and thirty by land, which he called Bolivar after the liberator of South America. This tract, of course, should not be confused with Bolivar Peninsula across the channel from Galveston. The distance from Bolivar to the navigable waters of Galveston Bay is considerably more than fifteen miles as estimated by Mrs. Holley. Henry's plan seemed to have been to purchase as much land as possible on credit with the assumption that he could sell some of his holdings and clear the remainder. This seems to be a rather devious method of doing business in a place where everyone was land poor; but Henry, like most of the Austins, did not appear to have a great deal of business ability. Henry professed to practice law and was evidently familiar with both Spanish and French as he often translated from either language. The following advertisement was from the *Advocate of the Peoples Rights* published in Brazoria, Texas, by Oliver H. Allen, February 22, 1834:

"Conveyancing & Translating
Henry Austin
Will draw and attend to the execution of DEEDS OF TRANSFER in due form of law. He
   will also TRANSLATE SPANISH AND FRENCH DOCUMENTS, at the usual charges.
   Citizens wishing his services will in his absence from town, please leave their notes of par-
   ticulars with Mr. Edmund Andrews, and they will be attended to promptly."

He did have the Austin diplomatic touch, and his greatest contribution to the history of Texas was the leadership that he contributed during the period when Stephen F. Austin was imprisoned in Mexico. His counsel, his writings and arguments during this period were directed toward a continuation of the conservative policy in dealing with Mexico which Stephen F. Austin had always advocated. His influence was far reaching.

During his later years, Henry Austin occasionally practiced law, although there is little indication that he took a very prominent position at the bar. He fought against indebtedness all his life, but when he died he did leave some property to his heirs.

No better description of the man could be found than the one he gives of himself in the first part of his holographic will:

". . . By this instrument written with my own hand on this the twenty-sixth day of April A. D. 1851 in the City of Galveston with the intent of making it serve as my last will and Testament be it known that I Henry Austin born in New Haven, Connecticut on the 31st day of January A. D. 1782 of Elijah Austin and his wife Esther Phelps and resident in Texas during the past twenty years being at this time in sound mind tho afflicted with disease the burden of nearly seventy years and a long period of indescribable misery from the persecution of Creditors for debts the revolution and advances and expenses for public service have involved me in, being desirous that any Estate shall be settled by gentlemen in whose probity I have implicit confidence that my debts may be discharged and some portion of my Estate acquired by a long life of incessant enterprise toil and privation and suffering may inure to my children . . ."
(The Last Will and Testament of Henry Austin, Galveston County Probate Records, Cause No. 233.)

27. See Sketch #1 on Bolivar.

28. We can assume that Mrs. Holley had arrived at Orizimbo, the plantation of Dr. James Aeneas E. Phelps which gained fame when it served as the prison of Santa Anna from July until November of 1836. The following story about Santa Anna is probably as accurate as many others which have been related by historians, particularly about his girl friends at San Antonio and San Jacinto:
"The plantation home of Dr. J. A. E. Phelps was developed as a cotton plantation, and well

improved as such. It is chiefly noted as the place where Gen. Santa Anna was kept as a prisoner of war. While there under guard, a soldier attempted to kill Santa Anna, and but for the timely action of Mrs. Phelps would have succeeded. In an instant she threw her arms around Santa Anna, which prevented the soldier from firing. This act saved his life. After this, Santa Anna attempted to take his life by poison, but the prompt action of Dr. Phelps in pumping the poison from him again saved his life. Santa Anna was a Mason, and it is said that it was largely the reason of his life having been spared. Sam Houston, the Whartons, Dr. Phelps, Wm. H. Patton and others of his captors were Masons. Santa Anna never forgot the kindness of Dr. Phelps and wife, and in later years when their son, Orlando, was taken prisoner in the ill-fated Mier expedition, Santa Anna showed his gratitude by setting Orlando free, as soon as he was notified that he was among the prisoners. He had him brought to the President's palace—kept him there some days, provided him with good clothes, paid his passage aboard ship to New York and gave him five hundred dollars in gold. This shows that good deeds do not always go unrewarded." (*The Old Plantations and their Owners of Brazoria County* by Abner J. Strobel; Houston: Union National Bank, 1930, pp. 34–35.)

The Phelps plantation was on the west side of the Brazos across from Henry Austin's plantation, which was a part of the William Harris Survey, Abstract #71.

REFERENCES:

Carlos E. Castañeda, *Our Catholic Heritage in Texas 1519–1936* (Austin: Von-Boeckmann-Jones, Co., 1936), Vol. VI.
Carlos E. Castañeda, *The Mexican Side of the Revolution* (Dallas: P. I. Turner Co., 1928).
Frank C. Hanighen, *The Napoleon of the West, Santa Anna* (Coward-McCann, Inc., 1934).
Wilfred H. Calcott, *Santa Anna: The Story of an Enigma Who Once Was Mexico* (Norman: University of Oklahoma Press, 1936).

29. The two nieces were Henrietta and Emily. They spent a good deal of time with Mrs. Holley, both in Texas and Lexington.

30. Green B. Jameson was born in Kentucky and, according to Mrs. Holley, attended school at Transylvania College. By October 1830, he was practicing law at San Felipe de Austin. He lived with Dr. Phelps for a short time before joining James Bowie at the Alamo as ensign and chief engineer. He died in the fall of the Alamo on March 6, 1836.

REFERENCES:

Biographical Notebooks, L. W. Kemp Collection, University of Texas Archives.

31. No record appears in the Deed Records of Brazoria County of the town of Orizimbo. We can at least credit the Phelps with finding an unusual name.

32. The widow Alsbury was Leah Alsbury, the widow of Thomas Alsbury, one of the Old Three Hundred, who was granted two leagues of land adjoining the Phelps' Orizimbo plantation on the north, in both Fort Bend and Brazoria counties. Thomas Alsbury had extensive holding at an early date, but died intestate in 1826 and left ten children and his widow. (Cause #11, Probate Records of Brazoria County, Texas, Thomas Alsbury, Deceased.) One of his sons signed the following advertisements:

"Notice of Second sale of lots in town of Montezuma," signed T. J. Alsberry. (*The Texas Republican,* April 4, 1835.)

From the *Telegraph and Texas Register,* Houston, Texas, November 18, 1837:

"Town of Monticello—The proprietor of this town-site offers the same to a discriminating public with the full conviction of its natural advantages and superiority of location in a commercial as well as geographical point of view—This place is situated on the West bank of the Brazos

River—Its geographical location is about equi-distant between Velasco and San Felipe—Between Matagorda and Houston—and from Galveston to Columbus—The Proprietor had laid off 1000 acres of land, including the town site and out lots, which he proposed to dispose of in shares, it being part of two leagues of land granted to Thomas Alsbury, by the Mexican Government in 1824, and one of the first selections.

Nov. 3, 1837   T. J. Alsbury"

Evidently, by 1837 Monticello was a much more popular name than Montezuma in Texas. The advertisements were run several years after the original grant.

33. The two Marys were Mary Trailer Austin, wife of Henry Austin, and their daughter Mary. William Ransom Hogan, the biographer of Henry Austin, was not sure of the date of the death of the daughter. This was probably because she had returned to New Orleans with Mrs. Holley after her visit in 1832. Mrs. Holley does not leave much doubt that both Marys died in the cholera epidemic in 1833. The old cemetery at Bolivar, where the two Marys were buried, cannot be located.

REFERENCES:

William Ransom Hogan, *op. cit.*, p. 69.
Eugene C. Barker, *op. cit.*, 1922, p. 154 (letter from Stephen F. Austin to Mary Austin Holley referring to the death, April 20, 1833).
J. Villasana Haggard, *op. cit.*, p. 317.
Letter from Mr. F. W. Turner to J. P. Bryan, June 1964 (J. P. Bryan Collection).

34. Mrs. Holley was fascinated with the bees and bee trees in Texas and wrote on this subject at some length:

"The forests of Texas are visited by numerous swarms of bees, which deposit their luscious stores in their hollow trees, and thus give rise to a profitable branch of trade in which many individuals are employed, viz: the sale of honey and wax, which are and will be important items of commerce. It is a very curious fact in the natural history of the bee, that it is never found in a wild country, but always precedes civilization, forming a kind of advance guard between the white man and the savage. The Indians, at least, are perfectly convinced of the truth of this fact, for it is a common remark among them, when they observe these happy and industrious insects, "there come the white men."

(*Texas* by Mary Austin Holley, p. 106.)

REFERENCES:

Mattie Austin Hatcher, *Mary Austin Holley* (Dallas: Southwest Press), p. 119.

35. Colonel Thomas Handasyd Perkins was a wealthy Bostonian, who "collected objects d'art," and entertained the Holleys when they stayed there. Likewise, Benjamin Bussey was a wealthy Bostonian who had a beautiful country estate outside Boston and was a good friend of the Holley family.

REFERENCES:

Lee, *op. cit.*, pp. 74, 93.

36. It is hard to believe that there was much sea breeze at Orizimbo, which is at least thirty miles from the coast.

37. A rather unusual dinner to say the least.

38. Evidently the event that Mrs. Holley refers to was the capture, on May 9th, of the *Columbia* by the Mexican warship *Montezuma*.

"Passengers present (in San Felipe) who were on board the Martha which was taken by the

Mexican armed vessel Montasume May 3rd and likewise some who were on board the Columbia captured by the same vessel on the 9th."

"And a rumor was abroad that while on her way to Vera Cruz, the Moctezuma (sic) had stopped at Velasco, and finding there the merchant ship Columbia, also who had no clearance papers, had captured her too."

("The Journal of Ammon Underwood, 1834–1838," edited by James K. Greer, *The Southwestern Historical Quarterly*, XXXII, p. 134.)

REFERENCES:

Eugene C. Barker, "Difficulties of a Mexican Revenue Officer in Texas," *Quarterly of the Texas State Historical Association*, IV, p. 193.

39. Mrs. Holley's condemnation of McKinney shows the strong influence of her conservative brother and the Empresario, her cousin. The partnership of McKinney and Williams has been noted earlier. They were inclined to be rather aggressive businessmen. Although Mrs. Holley is critical of McKinney because of his smuggling activities, Stephen F. Austin was probably much more concerned with his real estate dealings.

40. One of the interesting aspects of Bolivar is that it is located at the head of tidewater in the Brazos River and, although the river is usually fresh (at least on the surface), salt water fish are caught regularly at this point. (See Notes #145 and #196.)

41. Daughter, of course, is Harriette Holley Brand.

REFERENCES:

Letters of Mary Austin Holley, The University of Texas Archives.
Crosby Papers, Estate of the late Mrs. Benjamin Crosby, Spring Station, Kentucky.
Aldrich Collection, Mrs. Harriette Holley Aldrich, New York.
Transylvania College Library, Lexington, Kentucky.

42. This is the second man that Mrs. Holley met who died at the Alamo. Amos Pollard was born in Ashburnham, Massachusetts, on October 23, 1803. He received his medical training in New York and came to Texas in 1834, settling near Gonzales. Appointed by Stephen F. Austin as surgeon of the Texas Volunteer Army, he remained in San Antonio after its capture and was in the Alamo when it fell.

43. Rattlesnakes are still around and the sound that they make with their rattles could somewhat resemble a hissing.

44. It would appear that Mrs. Holley had several boring days.

45. This was one of the frequent periods when Mary Holley and her brother were suffering severe financial reversals. It would not be wrong to assume that Mary Austin Holley had come on this trip expecting to see her cousin Stephen F. Austin, and there are strong indications that they might have seriously contemplated matrimony. This might also have been an occasion when Mrs. Holley was feeling her age. She was born in 1784 and was at this time fifty-one years old. Austin's feeling regarding Mrs. Holley was shown in many of his letters; particularly in the following letter to Samuel May Williams dated April 2, 1831:

"I also want a good tract for Mrs. Holly, widow of the late Doctor Holly, who will remove to the Colony next fall certain, and be the most valuable acquisition we have ever yet received in the female line, or will receive." (*The Austin Papers*, 1922, II, 638.)

This middle-aged infatuation was noted by a good many writers, and Ellen Garwood (Mrs. St. John Garwood) of Austin, Texas, wrote a play on the subject.

REFERENCES:

Mary Austin Holley, *loc. cit.*

Eugene C. Barker, *op. cit.,* 1922, II, pp. 274, 725, 727, 736, 753 (letters from Stephen F. Austin to Mary Austin Holley), p. 275 (letter from Stephen F. Austin to Emily Margaret Perry), and p. 726 (letter from Stephen F. Austin to James F. Perry).

Ellen Garwood, "No Other Time for Austin" (original in possession of Mrs. Garwood).

46. The following advertisement appeared in the *Texas Republican,* February 14, 1835:
"The Schooner Santiago arrived at the mouth of the Brazos with several cases of small-pox on board."

47. The only available information about Applewhite is the following advertisement that was run in the *Texas Republican Newspaper,* June 11, 1835:
"Notice that Dr. Arthur Applewhite has located in Brazoria."
It is interesting to note that in the same paper there was the following advertisement:
"Notice of auction sale of furniture of July 15 at Bolivar by Henry Austin."

REFERENCES:

J. P. Bryan, *op. cit.,* I, pp. 69–70.

48. The area that Mrs. Holley describes is a portion of the S. F. Austin 7 1/3-League Grant which, from the time of its purchase in 1835 by the Crosby family, has been known as Crosby's Prairie. At the Crosby homesite, on the west side of the Brazos, there was a ferry crossing and boat landing. This local point eventually acquired the name of Perry's Landing. The Post Office, which for years was several miles inland and up the river, was known as Perry's Landing; evidently, taking the name from the place where the mail was first delivered from the boats in this area. The ferry was permanently abandoned in 1915 or 1916. The Crosbys still own a portion of the original tract and at least one member of the family (Walter Crosby) lives in close proximity.

49. Mrs. Perry was Emily Margaret Austin, daughter of Moses Austin and sister of Stephen F. Austin. She was born in Austinville, Virginia, in 1795. Emily Margaret had attended The Hermitage (a school for young ladies) in New York and had a fairly good education for a young woman who had spent most of her life in the frontier area of the country. Her mother, Maria Brown Austin, brought her to Kentucky in 1804, and it was while she was attending Mrs. Beck's Boarding School that she met her cousin, Mary Austin Holley. At this time, her father's fortunes began to wane and she returned to the Austin home in Potosi, Missouri, and married James Bryan on August 13, 1813. They had three children who reached maturity: W. Joel, Moses Austin, and Guy M. James Bryan had made extensive plans to join Stephen F. Austin in Texas. Certificates to locate land were given to the victims of an earthquake in the town of New Madrid in Upper Louisiana, and Stephen F. Austin and James Bryan purchased several of these certificates. James Bryan attempted to locate one at what is now the present town of Little Rock, Arkansas; however, the title to the grant was defective and the venture failed. James Bryan died in 1822 and left Emily Margaret a widow with four small children. At this time, one catastrophe followed another in her life. Her father had died shortly before, and her mother died in 1824. Her situation was critical, and for a while she taught school to support her children.

In 1824, she married James F. Perry, who was a successful merchant in Potosi, Missouri. Austin wrote to his sister on several occasions urging the family to come to Texas. They finally arrived in 1831, having been recipients of one of the eleven-league grants. This property, lying between Pleasant and Chocolate Bayous in Brazoria County, makes up a large part of what is known as the Chocolate Bayou Oil Field. Perry and his son, Stephen S. Perry, conducted a ranching operation on the property for many years, but the permanent home was at Peach Point on a 1,908 ½ acre tract that Perry purchased from Stephen F. Austin, and upon which he began the development of the plantation in 1832.

When James F. Perry first arrived in Texas, he opened a store at San Felipe de Austin and had as his associates William W. Hunter and Alexander Somervell. Emily Margaret accompanied her husband to Texas with her family, which now numbered six. Her infant daughter (Mary Bryan), who died in 1833, was the first person buried in the old Peach Point Cemetery or Gulf Prairie Cemetery. Perry and Emily Margaret had three children who reached maturity: Stephen Samuel, Henry Austin, and Eliza. Eliza was not well mentally and her father took her, in 1853, to Biloxi, Mississippi, for treatment; he also planned to meet his son Henry, who had just graduated from Trinity College in Connecticut. Within a week, both the father and son died of yellow fever. Their burial place has never been located.

Yellow fever was a scourge of the Austin family. Elijah, Mary Austin Holley's father, died of it in Connecticut; James E. B. Austin, Stephen F. Austin's brother, died of yellow fever in New Orleans in 1829; Horace Holley died of yellow fever contracted in 1827; and Mary Austin Holley died of it in New Orleans in 1846.

James F. Perry was successful in operating his Peach Point plantation, and a detailed account of this operation has been recorded. (See Abigail Curlee, *The Southwestern Historical Quarterly,* XXVI, 79.) After Stephen F. Austin's death, Emily Margaret Perry inherited a large portion of his property running into many thousands of acres. In Brazoria County today in the vicinity of Peach Point (or rather the lower part of Brazoria County), her heirs still own much of the property left her, and the list of her descendants from both the Perry and Bryan families, is so numerous that it requires the talent of an historian to keep up with them. Emily Margaret died at Peach Point on August 15, 1851.

REFERENCES:

Lela E. McKinley, "Life of James F. Perry" (Master's Thesis, University of Texas, 1934).
Adele Perry Caldwell (great-great granddaughter of Emily Margaret Perry), "Genealogy of the Perry Family" (MS. in possession of the author in Freeport, Texas).
J. Perry Moore, "Heirs of Emily Margaret Austin" (copy of MS. in possession of J. P. Bryan).
Mrs. Guy Adriance (nee Lois Brock) & Mrs. John Caldwell (nee Adele Perry) "Heirship of Genealogy of the James Bryan Family" (MS. in possession of authors).
See Note #140 for reference to law suit.

50. The two hundred acres that Mrs. Holley talks about seem to have been a matter of great concern to her from the period of her first visit, when she met Stephen F. Austin at Bolivar, in 1831. The following is quoted from Stephen F. Austin's letter to her on January 4, 1832:

"Your brother Henry is authorized to chuse[sic?] a situation for you out of my 'Peach Point' survey of premium land—say two hundred acres. I expect to be back soon enough to designate it myself before it will be necessary to begin building, and should prefer doing so, but if I am detained too long he can make a selection. Farewell." *(The Austin Papers,* II, 733.)

Austin had also arranged for her to have a league on Dickinson Bayou in present Galveston County, but he did not make any formal conveyance to her of any of the so-called premium land. He did remember her in his will, and she received a league of land on Flores Bayou in Brazoria County, Texas, which was worth a good many times the proposed two hundred acres. Mrs. Perry deeded to Mary Austin Holley two lots at Quintana (Deed

Records of Brazoria County, Texas, March 1, 1838), and there is some indication that this was intended to assuage her disappointment because she did not receive the premium land.

REFERENCES:

Lee, *op. cit.,* p. 399.
Will of Stephen F. Austin, Probate Records of Brazoria County, Texas.

51. Mrs. Sayre was the wife of Charles D. Sayre, who was prominent in the early affairs of Brazoria County. Early records of Brazoria County show numerous real estate transactions and other legal matters which involved Charles D. Sayre. (See Note #68 for additional information on Charles D. Sayre.)

52. Miss McNeel was Elizabeth McNeel, one of the daughters of John McNeel. She later married Robert Mills (See Note #162.)

53. Bevil Census of 1935 listed Barney Low, who had a nineteen-year-old daughter named Peggy Ann. Whether or not this is the same family is purely conjecture.

54. This may be the best description of Velasco and the mouth of the river that has been preserved. (See Sketches #1, 2 & 3).

55. Mrs. Holley gives us little information about the newly landed Africans, but it would appear that these were slaves who had been imported from Cuba or some other foreign country. Needless to say, this was an illegal transaction, but it seems to have been carried on by some of the most prominent members of Austin's colony. It may well have been that the slaves whom Mrs. Holley saw were imported by J. W. Fannin, the commander at Goliad. The following is from an article by Eugene C. Barker, "The African Slave Trade in Texas," *Quarterly of the Texas State Historical Association,* VI, p. 152: "It is also said that J. W. Fannin brought a hundred Africans to Texas in 1835." Other prominent slave traders whom Mrs. Holley met while in Texas were Sterling McNeel and Benjamin Fort Smith.

56. Mrs. Holley's talents included the writing of poems and lyrics for songs. The song she referred to is probably "Pensez à moi" composed by James G. Drake.

REFERENCES:

Music Division, Library of Congress, Letter to Ford Dixon, December, 1964.

57. Dr. Cook could have been the originator of a popular medicine of the time, Cook's Pills, as in Carter's Little Liver Pills. For Captain Hurd, see Note #1. We have no information regarding Captain Hutton other than that he was captain of the *Julius Caesar* (consistently misspelled by Mrs. Holley in the diary).

58. Captain Fuller of the San Felipe. (See Note #1).

59. This is a reference to Sarah Kemble Siddons, eighteenth-century actress. Mrs. Holley might have been referring to one of two books: James Boaden's *Memoirs of Mrs. Siddons,* published in London in 1827, or Thomas Cambell's *Life of Mrs. Siddons,* published in London in 1834.

60. As has been noted elsewhere, for at least a time Stephen F. Austin and Mary Austin Holley seem to have had a strong romantic attachment, and it would appear that they did plan some future life in Texas. At this time Austin's only close relatives were his nephew, Stephen F. Austin, Jr., the son of James E. B. Austin; and his sister, Emily Margaret Perry; and these two persons became his principal beneficiaries. Although Emily and Mary visited on several occasions and at times seemed to be on friendly terms, it is doubtful that the

two women were ever very close. It is obvious that Mrs. Holley's life in Texas would have been much better had Austin lived.

REFERENCES:

Lee, *op. cit.,* p. 238.
Barker, *op. cit.,* 1922, II, 72 (Stephen F. Austin to James F. Perry, December 27, 1931).
Ibid., 1919, II, 322 (New Madrid land certificate) 336 (real estate advertisement), and 358–59, 363–64 (letters from Stephen F. Austin to James Bryan).

61. Mrs. Holley's continuing battle with seasickness. Traveling by boat at that time would have been bad enough for a man, but it must have been a real ordeal for a woman.

62. The famous Balize lights are a series of channel markers and lighthouses set out to mark the mouth of the Mississippi River below New Orleans. Doubtless they were a welcome sight to the bad sailor Holley. For many years they have notified the sea-weary that port is near. Several sea chanties exist about them, describing the happiness of the sailor and his anticipation of the joys of New Orleans.

63. It would be interesting to know what a soda shop looked like in 1835—banana splits, sandwiches, chili?

64. St. Peter's Street in New Orleans refers to the town house of Mr. and Mrs. Hermogene Labranche. Mrs. Holley was governess to Melazie, the daughter, for many years.

REFERENCES:

Lee, *op. cit.,* p. 201. (See plates of the house following page 196).
Mattie Austin Hatcher, *op. cit.,* p. 29.

65. It was certainly not an impressive trip, and it must have been a disappointment not to have seen any new parts of the land.

66. One wonders what had happened to Natchez in the intervening years.

67. William Stafford came to Texas in 1822 as one of Austin's "Old Three Hundred" colonists and had received his original grant in Fort Bend and Waller Counties. He opened a plantation at an early period and was one of the first planters to produce sugar. Mrs. Dilue Harris, who was a young girl in February of 1834, recalled in later years:

"Mr. Stafford made sugar. His sugar was not under water. The sugar was as black as tar." ("Reminiscences of Mrs. Dilue Harris," *Quarterly of the Texas State Historical Association,* IV, 93.)

The sale of the Stafford Plantation as reported by Mrs. Holley may have been due to the fact that in June 1835, William Stafford killed a man named Moore and fled to the United States. The small town of Stafford, Texas, in Fort Bend County, approximately twenty miles from Houston, was originally named Stafford Point, the plantation home of William Stafford.

Mrs. Holley was always interested in getting a price on her land.

68. Charles D. Sayre was one of the early colonists in Brazoria County and was a successful planter and businessman. He had a large plantation at what is now known as Bailey's Prairie (See Sketch #7) which he operated with a great deal of efficiency. Sayre's ability as a planter must have been noted for many years, as P. A. Champonier reported that Charles D. Sayre produced 570 hogsheads of sugar on his Brazoria County plantation from 1852 through 1855. (See *A Short History of the Sugar Industry in Texas* by William R. Johnson.) At one time, he evidently owned the schooner *The Nelson* (registration of *The Nelson,* the National Archives, Washington, D. C.), which was active in Texas

trade for many years. There seems to be no information regarding the place of Sayre's birth, his wife's maiden name, or their family—if any. He is listed in the *Handbook of Texas,* and there is a biography of sorts in *Biographical Directory of the Texas Conventions and Congresses.* He appeared in Texas in the early 1830s and evidently dropped from public sight in the middle 1850s. An exchange of letters between Stephen F. Austin and Charles D. Sayre in 1832 indicates that they did not see eye to eye on events leading up to the Battle of Velasco. (See Walter E. Grover, "Correspondence Between Stephen F. Austin and Charles D. Sayre," *Southwestern Historical Quarterly,* LXIII, 454–56.) However, it would appear that by the time Mrs. Holley arrived in Texas in 1835 they were very friendly, as she was with the Sayres a good part of the time. Although Sayre seemed active in supporting the Battle of Velasco, the records do not indicate that he participated.

69. James Britain (Brit) Bailey is the person whom Mrs. Holley referred to, but her account of how he came to Texas is not generally a part of the record. He was in Texas before Stephen F. Austin arrived, and he was what might well have been termed "a character." One of the legends surrounding him is that he desired to be buried erect with his rifle by his side and a jug of whiskey at his feet.

"A noted member of Austin's colony was Captain James B. Bailey better known as Brit Bailey, his arrival even antedating that of Austin himself. But as up to that period foreigners could not procure title to land, Bailey had only squatter's claim. Still he felt that the priority of his claim should be respected; therefore he rose in rebellion when notified that his claim would have to comply with the regulations governing the real colonists. A compromise was effected, however, and Captain Bailey lived and died on his original claim. When he was in his last sickness, realizing that the end was near, he said to his wife:

" 'I have never stooped to any man, and when I am in my grave I don't want it said, 'There lies old Brit Bailey.' Bury me so that the world must say, 'There stands Bailey.' And bury me with my face to the setting sun. I have been all my life traveling westward and I want to face that way when I die.'

"His widow in compliance with his request, had a deep hole dug like a well into which the coffin was lowered, feet first, facing the setting sun." (*The Evolution of a State,* by Noah Smithwick, pp. 72–73.)

70. Washington Irving's "A Tour on the Prairies" is referred to by Mrs. Holley, Chapter Seven. This was written when Irving was on a trip with Charles Joseph Latrobe and Commissioner Henry L. Ellsworth.

REFERENCES:

Johnson, Malone, *op. cit.,* V, 510 (Washington Irving).

71. The reference to the Bay of Espiritu Santo introduces some nomenclature which was rather loosely used—at least for two hundred years of Texas history. When Piñeda first sailed the Gulf (1519), one of the points that he located on his map was Espiritu Santo, which obviously was the mouth of the Mississippi River. This name was shifted several hundred miles south, during the time of LaSalle's exploration in Texas, to the bay that lies behind Matagorda Island and is entered through present Pass Cavallo. The larger bay to the east is now known as Matagorda Bay but was called Lago de San Bernardo by the early Spaniards.

REFERENCES:

J. P. Bryan, Walter Hanak, *Texas in Maps* (Piñeda's Map of 1519), p. 22.
Map by Cardenas. 1691. J. P. Bryan Collection (Sketch of original located in the Archivo General de las Indias, Seville).

72. *Atkinson's Casket,* or *Gems of Literature* was published in Philadelphia from 1831

to 1839 by a man named Atkinson. This extract is from Vol. VIII, No. 9, September, 1833. Evidently Mrs. Holley reproduced this publication in her book *Texas*.

73. When Stephen F. Austin returned from prison in Mexico in August of 1835, he wrote a rather lengthy letter to Mrs. Holley in which he expressed his position at that time regarding Texas' future relations with Mexico. He concluded his letter with the following request:

"To conclude—I wish a great immigration this fall and winter from Kentucky, Tennessee, everywhere, passports, or no passports, any how. For fourteen years I have had a hard time of it, but nothing shall daunt my courage or abate my exertions to complete the main object of my labors—To Americanize Texas. This fall, and winter, will fix our fate—a great immigration will settle this question." (*The Austin Papers,* III, pp. 101–3.)

This is evidently a list of the material contributed to the companies of Kentucky soldiers, actually called Kentucky Emigrants, who were leaving for Texas during the early part of 1836. Mrs. Holley advertised in several papers at this time for supplies.

REFERENCES:

Lee, *op. cit., pp.* 272–73.
Hogan, *op. cit.,* p. 73.

74. The accounting is difficult to understand. We can assume that the proceeds from the book would be those for *Texas,* which was ready for sale by July of 1836. There were many Marys in the family, but her niece Mary Austin (daughter of Henry) was dead by this time. "Horace" was of course her son, who caused his mother a great deal of anxiety because evidently he was not of sound mind. This may have been a bill to her brother for the care of his children. During the early part of 1837, Mrs. Holley was in Lexington, Kentucky, and she did not leave until March to go to New Orleans. She then returned to Lexington in the summer. At that time, Emily Margaret Perry spent a month in Lexington, as she was on her way to put one of her sons in Kenyon College in Ohio. The son wrote:

"In the fall months and part of the Spring, my half brother Stephen and I went to school to a Mr. Copeland on Chocolate Bayou, place now known as Liverpool. On May 14th, 1837, I left with my mother and brother Austin and sister, Eliza, and Mr. Perry, from the mouth of the Brazos, in a brig for New Orleans.
"Mother and Austin accompanied my sister and myself on steamboat up the Mississippi to Louisville and thence to Lexington, Ky., where my mother and Uncle Stephen F. Austin had many friends, whose friendship they formed during their school days. Remaining there a month on a visit to Mrs. Holley (who was first cousin to my mother) and other friends we left for Louisville, where we spent several days meeting friends; thence we went to Portsmouth, Ohio, to visit with some relations of Mr. Perry; mother and sister remained there.
"My brother Austin and myself left on Canal Packet on Ohio & Erie Canal going as far as the town of Newark, where we took stage for Kennon College where I entered as a student; my brother returned in a day or two to my mother and sister. I remained there for five years and graduated."

(Memoirs of Guy M. Bryan, in possession of Mrs. Guy M. Bryan, 3402 Garrott, Houston, Texas.)

REFERENCES:

Lee, *op. cit.,* pp. 276–85, 288.

75. It appears that Mrs. Holley was fond of crackers and cheese. Evidently, these expenses and items refer to Mrs. Holley's third trip to Texas and should bear the date of December 1837. She arrived at Galveston before Christmas of that year.

REFERENCES:

Lee, *op. cit.*, 289–90.

76. "Wright's 'Gallery of National Portraits' hung in the Capitol Building for several weeks. Wright painted at least two portraits of Houston, whose willingness to pose in all sorts of costumes assured him recognition as being one of the most painted and photographed officials in the Western Hemisphere." (*Texas Avenue at Main Street* by A. Pat Daniels; Houston: Allen Press, 1964).

77. She sees a good bit of the President during her stay in Houston. Sam Houston was sworn in as the first president of the Republic of Texas on October 22, 1836, in Columbia, which was the first capital of the Republic. In December of 1836, the Congress passed an act locating the capital in Houston, which had been laid out by the Allen brothers, John Kirby and Augustus C., and named for the new President—even before his election. The Congress did not actually meet in Houston until May of 1837. This is probably the first time that Mrs. Holley had ever met General Sam Houston, and it seems that she had a good opinion of the President. After the Battle of San Jacinto, she had written a song dedicated to General Houston. The full title is "The Texas Song of Liberty."

REFERENCES:

Lee, *op. cit.*, 290–91.
A. Pat Daniels, *Texas Avenue at Main Street*, p. 3.

78. Henry Wax Karnes was in command of a small force at San Antonio at this time. He came to Texas from Arkansas and was active in most of the engagements during the Revolution. He and Erastus "Deaf" Smith were Houston's principal scouts during the retreat to San Jacinto.

   The war that Mrs. Holley refers to from time to time was another of the many false alarms that spread throughout Texas for the first two or three years after San Jacinto. There was no actual invasion of Texas by Mexican armies until March 1842, when General Rafael Vasquez took San Antonio. It was again captured by General Woll in September 1842.

REFERENCES:

Joseph Milton Nance, *After San Jacinto.*

79. The Mrs. Allen whom Mrs. Holley refers to, would be the wife of Augustus C. Allen, who with his bachelor brother, John Kirby Allen, founded the city of Houston. Mrs. Allen, formerly Charlotte Baldwin, evidently invested a good bit of her money in the Allens' enterprises involving the development of the city. The Allens built on Block 48, Lot 6, in Houston.

REFERENCES:

Edwin A. Bonewitz Letter to Ford Dixon, December 13, 1964 (affidavit of Charlotte Baldwin Allen given in the District Court of Harris County giving the site of her home in 1837 as Block 48, Lot 6).
Map of Houston, locating Block 48, Lot 6, at corner of Prairie Avenue & Caroline Street.

80. Alceé Louis Labranche, the United States chargé d'affaires to Texas, was the cousin of Hermogene Labranche, at whose home Mrs. Holley was a tutor for many years.

REFERENCES:

Lee, *op. cit.*, p. 291.
George P. Garrison (ed.), *Texas Diplomatic Correspondence* (Washington: Government

Printing Office 1908–1911).

81. It was obvious that the President had very poor quarters, at least initially, in Houston. It is a wonder that Sam Houston did not build on Block 43 which the Allens had given him.

REFERENCES:

Samuel Wood Geiser, *Naturalists of the Frontier* (Dallas: Southern Methodist Press, 1948), pp. 79–84.

M. K. Wisehart, *Sam Houston, American Giant* (Washington: Robert B. Luce, Inc., 1962), pp. 298–99.

A. Pat Daniels, *op. cit.*, p. 1.

82. Mrs. McCormick was Peggy McCormick, the widow of Arthur McCormick, one of Austin's "Old Three-Hundred." It was on her league of land that the Battle of San Jacinto was fought. When complaining to Houston about the pile of dead Mexicans on her land, she is reported to have said, "To the Devil with your glorious history."

REFERENCES:

Frank X. Tolbert, *The Day of San Jacinto* (New York: McGraw-Hill Book Co., Inc., 1959), p. 201.

Biographical Notebooks, L. W. Kemp Collection, University of Texas Archives.

83. The places referred to are well-known locations either along Buffalo Bayou, West Bay, or the San Jacinto River. Clappers probably refers to Clopper's Point on Galveston Bay.

84. The cost-of-living index was obviously pretty high at this time.

85. See Sketches #8, 9, 10A, 10B, and 11 of Houston scenes.

86. Captain George Washington Wheelright was an officer in the Texas Navy, during the periods of both the Revolution and the Republic.

REFERENCES:

Hill, *op. cit.*, p. 74.

Dienst, *op. cit.*, p. 37.

87. Evidently Mrs. Holley refers to Moseley Baker, who at one time lived in the Houston-Galveston area and in 1839 (in the Campaign against the Indians) had the rank of Brigadier General. Captain Moseley Baker was one of the Texas officers who refused to follow Houston in his earlier retreat across the Brazos.

REFERENCES:

H. Yoakum, *History of Texas* (Austin: The Steck Company, 1935), p. 41.

Tolbert, *op. cit.*, p. 52.

88. Mrs. Bee was Anne Bee, the wife of Barnard E. Bee who played an important part in the early history of Texas. He had been Secretary of War, but had resigned prior to Mrs. Holley's arrival. Bee was the brother-in-law of the famous governor of South Carolina, James Hamilton, who spent a great deal of his time and money in attempting to gain recognition of Texas by foreign powers and also to secure financial aid for the young Republic. Among other things, James Hamilton opened the Retrieve plantation in Brazoria County, part of which is out of the Jared E. Groce 5-League Grant, which was one of the largest plantations during the early period of the Republic. (See information under Sketches 15 and 16.) Barnard E. Bee was one of the Texans selected to escort Santa Anna to the United

States, and Mrs. Holley had occasion to see him in Lexington in December of 1837. (See Note #10.)

Bee's greatest claim to fame may have been the fact that he was the father of Hamilton Prioleau Bee, who was a Confederate general from Texas and is famous for the following remark at the First Battle of Manassas:

"There is Jackson standing like a stone wall. Let us determine to die here, and we will conquer. Follow me."

(*Mighty Stonewall* by Frank Vandiver; see Sketch #10A of the Bee home.)

REFERENCE:

Lee, *op. cit.*, p. 279–80.

89. John Birdsall was born in New York. His family migrated to Texas in 1829. By 1837, he was practicing law with Thomas J. Gazley. Sam Houston appointed him Attorney General of the Republic on August 15, 1837. In 1838, his appointment as Chief Justice of the Supreme Court, pro tem, was turned down by the Texas Senate and he returned to private life. He died on July 22, 1839. Myron and Orville Holley were two brothers of Mrs. Holley's husband.

90. This is Edwin Morehouse, who in the fall and winter of 1835–36, went to New York to recruit volunteers for Texas. From October 1836 to June 1837, he represented Goliad, Refugio, and San Patricio Counties in the Senate. He was Brigadier General of the Militia and had considerable experience as an Indian fighter, leading expeditions up the Brazos in 1838–1839.

91. Mrs. Holley's observation about the terrain would fit today. Even with ditches, it is still difficult to drain flat land. (See map of Highway 288, page 72.)

92. There is no way of identifying which lake Mrs. Holley refers to, as there are many throughout this area.

93. Francis Bingham was one of Austin's "Original Three Hundred" and was granted a league which is now on the boundary line between Fort Bend and Brazoria Counties. When the counties were surveyed, Francis Bingham was determined to see that his league remained in Brazoria County.

"In 1837 when Moses Lapham was riding the survey lines for Fort Bend County, the first survey called to cross the river at Alsbury's League at the mouth of Cow Creek which was to be the south line of the County west of the Brazos. This would have taken Bigham (Bingham) and several other Oyster Creek leagurers east of the river from Brazoria and included them in Fort Bend. Old Francis objected. He said he had lived in Brazoria ever since he came to Texas, that he liked the climate and the water and his neighbors, that he never did like the Fort Bend County climate—it was hotter in the summer colder in the winter, wetter in the spring. He talked the locators into sticking to the old Harrisburg County line which made his upper line the southline of Fort Bend east of the Brazos and left him in old Brazoria." (*History of Fort Bend County* by Clarence R. Wharton; San Antonio: Naylor Press, 1939, p. 35.)

A part of the Bingham League (Abstract #43) in Brazoria County, Texas, is still owned by the heirs of Francis Bingham. None resides on the plantation, but there are heirs living in Brazoria and Harris Counties—principally, the Joe B. Tigner and John H. (Tim) Tigner families, and Mrs. Armour Munson of Houston.

REFERENCE:

Abner J. Strobel, *The Old Plantations and Their Owners of Brazoria County, Texas* (Houston: Union National Bank, 1930).

94. It would be impossible to know where Mrs. Holley was at this time, or what plantation she might be referring to. (See map of Highways 288 and 35 from Houston to Columbia and Brazoria.)

95. The Brazoria County Chamber of Commerce would probably be happy to have Mrs. Holley's observations.

96. Colonel Fisher was probably William S. Fisher, who came to Texas from Virginia in 1834, represented the municipality of Gonzales at the Consultation at San Felipe in 1835, participated in the battle of San Jacinto, and served as Secretary of War of the Republic from December 1836 until November 1837. Appointed lieutenant colonel in 1837 of a frontier cavalry regiment Fisher later took part in the Mier Expedition, was wounded and imprisoned. Released in 1843, he returned to his home in Jackson County, Texas, where he died in 1845.

John Grant Tod was born in Lexington, Kentucky, in 1809. He became Captain of the Texas Navy in 1836, and later, Naval Agent in New Orleans. He purchased Mrs. Holley's Dickinson Bayou League (located between the present towns of Dickinson and Arcadia in Galveston County, Texas) for the cited consideration of $2,000, which was evidently about a quarter of what Mrs. Holley thought her property was worth. There are several letters in the Tod Collection at the University of Texas regarding the sale of the property. Mrs. Holley received her grant from the Government of Texas and Coahuila on June 13, 1831. Her conveyance to John Grant Tod is dated April 7, 1841, and is recorded in Book Two of the Deed Records of Galveston County, Texas. Mrs. Holley is referred to as Mary Ann Austin, the Widow Holley.

REFERENCES:

L. W. Kemp's Notes on the Holley Diary, Mary Austin Holley Collection, University of Texas Archives.

San Jacinto Notebooks, The L. W. Kemp Collection, University of Texas Archives.

97. Back with our old friends the Andrews (see Note #20).

98. Texana on the Navidad was at one time known as Santa Anna, and although no longer in existence was near the present town of Edna in Jackson County.

99. The Colonel Seguin referred to would have been Juan Seguin, son of the better known Erasmus of San Antonio, a close associate of Stephen F. Austin's. Juan Seguin at this time was held in high repute by Texas Government but later defected to the Mexican side. The Seguin family history is almost a history of Texas in itself.

100. Edwards Point was the original name of the townsite of San Leon, Galveston County. It is a finger of land extending into Galveston Bay, two and one-fourth miles north of the point where Dickinson Bayou joins the bay. It was doubtless considered a valuable area because of its easy access to shipping.

REFERENCE:

U. S. Coastal Survey Map, 1851, University of Texas Archives.

101. Mrs. Holley is again referring to Charles D. Sayre and the produce from his plantation on the Brazos River near Brazoria. (See Note #68 & Sketch #7 on Sayre.)

102. Mrs. Holley had previously approached Emily Margaret Perry about writing the memoirs of Stephen F. Austin, and had been informed that the family intended to have Lamar do it. Lamar at this time was Vice-President of the Republic of Texas and was soon to be elected its second president. Although he did not write the life of Austin, he did spend

a great deal of time collecting historical material on early Texas, and his papers, *The Papers of Mirabeau Buonaparte Lamar,* are considered a must item by all students of Texas history. (See *Mary Austin Holley* by Rebecca Smith Lee, pages 292–93, concerning a conversation between Lamar and Mrs. Holley regarding the biography of Stephen F. Austin.)

REFERENCE:

Herbert Pickens Gambrell, *Mirabeau Buonaparte Lamar, Troubadour and Crusader* (Dallas: Southwest Press, 1934).

103. Colonel Alexander Somervell, who was at one time a partner in the mercantile business with James F. Perry at San Felipe de Austin, was one of the most active leaders in the Texas Army during the early stages of the Republic. (In 1842 he commanded the troops that were sent to relieve the Siege of San Antonio, his orders from President Houston being not to pursue the enemy beyond the Rio Grande. He obeyed these orders, but other leaders, William S. Fisher and Thomas J. Green, decided to attack the Mexicans on the west side of the Rio Grande. As a result of this misadventure, we have the stories of the Mier Expedition and the prisoners of Perote to add to the annals of Texas history.)

REFERENCES:

General Thomas J. Green, *Journal of the Texian Expedition Against Mier* (New York: Harper & Bros., 1945.)

William P. Stapp, "The Prisoners of Perote" (LaGrange, Texas: *LaGrange Journal,* 1933.)

104. The only information we have concerning the Blandins is that they had a store in Brazoria. We cannot be sure that the place they were staying was at, or near, the location of John Austin's store referred to in Note #21. Part of this building, which was evidently constructed in 1828, was standing until a few years ago when it was demolished by the owners.

105. Brother Henry's business was bad as usual. His financial sufferings would equal the tribulations of Job.

106. Mrs. Holley seems to be showing quite an attachment for the grape.

107. Again, Mrs. Holley is fooled by the unusualness of Texas weather.

108. Mrs. Polley was Augusta, daughter of James Britain Bailey of Bailey's Prairie fame (see Note #69) who married Joseph H. Polley. Polley was with Austin on his first trip to San Antonio in 1821. He was a successful cattleman while in Brazoria but later moved his operations to the west and located on Cibolo Creek, where his cattle could run all the way to the Rio Grande. He was credited at the time of his death in 1869 with having the most extensive herds in Texas. Mexican bandits drove away more than 16,000 head of cattle but he still had more than 150,000 left. Joseph Polley left many heirs, some of whom now live in Harris and Fort Bend Counties: Dr. Hampton C. Robinson of Houston; Mrs. George Carmack of Houston; and Hampton C. Robinson, Sr. of Richmond, Texas.

Probably Mrs. Bowen was the widow of Sylvester Bowen, who was an early settler of Brazoria County and participated in the Battle of Velasco. He died in 1837, and probate proceedings were held on his estate in Brazoria County. Heirs of Sylvester Bowen and his widow still own an undivided interest in 428 acres of the original tract which is a part of the Asa Mitchell League, Abstract #97, and located on Bailey's Prairie.

REFERENCES:

Sylvester and Amanda Bowles Bowen heirship chart, compiled by the Brazoria County Abstract Office.

Probate Cases filed in Texas: Estate of Sylvester Bowen, Deceased, Cause No. 42, 1837.

109. A reference to the poem by William Cowper, "The Diverting History of John Gilpin; Showing How He Went Farther Than He Intended and Came Safe Home Again."

110. In 1821, Moses Austin had obtained tentative approval for a colonization project in Texas and it was his request, before his death, that the endeavor be carried on by his son, Stephen. Stephen had attended Transylvania College in Lexington, Kentucky, with one Littleberry Hawkins, a brother of Joseph H. Hawkins, with whom Stephen F. Austin was living in New Orleans when Moses Austin died and who had been prominent in the affairs of the State of Kentucky before coming to New Orleans. In order to finance a portion of the expenses of the original colony, Austin had agreed to give Joseph Hawkins a half interest in the venture. The extent of Hawkins' investment in the joint venture is not clear, as he and Austin did not agree on the amount; however, he did make a substantial contribution to the outfitting of the little boat that the partners purchased in New Orleans (the *Lively*) and also to Austin's overland trip to the mouth of the Colorado River (San Bernardo). It was contemplated that the *Lively* would carry settlers to the port of Austin's colony and that he would meet them there to establish a permanent settlement. As we note later, this endeavor was never completed.

Hawkins died in New Orleans in 1824 and at the time of his death was destitute, having lost his fortune in Texas in speculative affairs not concerned with Stephen F. Austin. Later, Austin partitioned the land granted to him for settling the original three hundred families in Texas, and the Hawkins heirs were allotted the 22 1/2 leagues and 3 labors of land (being approximately 100,000 acres), a large portion being located in Brazoria County. The property mentioned by Mrs. Holley was a portion of the Hawkins estate which is in the Stephen F. Austin 5-League Grant, Abstract #19, on the west bank of the Brazos River.

REFERENCES:

Tyler's Quarterly, history and genealogy magazine, Vol. 3, pp. 2–23, July, 1921.
For a short biography of Joseph Hawkins, see map of Brazoria County: Stephen F. Austin 5-League Grant, Abstract #19; Stephen F. Austin 7 1/2 League Grant, Abstract #20.
Partition Deed of Stephen F. Austin to Joseph Hawkins, Spanish Records, p. 57, of Deed Records of Brazoria County.
Barker, *op. cit.,* 1922, II., pp. 883–84.
Barker, *op. cit.,* pp. 251–52.

111. Evidently a good description of Lamar. A great deal was written about the activties of the early leaders of Texas history, but few writers gave any personal description.

112. The editor has not been able to obtain any information regarding an offer on the part of the Coushatta Indians to take part in the war on the Texan side. The Coushattas and the Alabamas, closely related tribes, were living at this time on the Trinity and Neches Rivers. These Indians were agrarian and were definitely friendly to the Texans. Their friendship was rewarded by the passage of the Relief Bill for their benefit by the Fourth Congress of Texas in 1841. In 1854, primarily through the efforts of Sam Houston, the land for a reservation near Livingston (Polk County) was purchased and granted to the Indians, and the few survivors reside there today.

REFERENCE:

W. W. Newcomb, Jr., *Indians of Texas* (Austin: University of Texas Press, 1961, pp. 24, 319.

113. Brazoria remained the county seat from 1837 until 1896, when the seat was finally relocated at Angleton.

REFERENCE:

Frank K. Stevens, "Memoirs of Seventy-Eight Years in Brazoria County" (*Angleton Times*, 1964).

114. Colonel James Love was an attorney from Kentucky, with whom Mrs. Holley had some dealings in connection with her Texas lands. He married Lucy Ballinger in Kentucky and came to Texas in 1837, settling first in Houston and later in Galveston. The Ballinger family is still prominent in Galveston County. Colonel Love became an extensive land owner in Brazoria County and took an active interest in politics. It would not be wrong to say that he was dedicated to the cause of the Confederacy, as at the age of sixty-six he enlisted in Terry's Texas Rangers.

REFERENCE:

Lee, *op. cit.*, 286.

115. See Sketch #12 on Peach Point.

116. *Norma* is of course the opera by Bellini.

117. See previous Note #49 on Bryan-Perry families.

118. It is doubtful if anyone could see the gulf from Peach Point in a normal house. (See Sketch #12 of Peach Point.)

119. The hill referred to is only a high ridge, obviously formed by some action of the Brazos River, which is a distance of about a mile and a half. The Peach Point home was built on the edge of the ridge, which would likewise be the edge of the forest, and was faced south so that it would have the benefit of the gulf breezes.

120. James Beard was with Austin on his first trip to Texas in July of 1821. He was known as the saddlemaker. (See Austin's Journal in *the Quarterly of the Texas State Historical Association*, VII, 286.

It is very possible that he did come from Missouri to Texas with Moses Austin. He is definitely listed as one of the group who came with Stephen F. Austin on his first exploratory journey to Texas.

REFERENCES:

A. J. Sowell, *History of Fort Bend County* (Houston: W. H. Coyle & Co., 1904.)
Wharton, *op. cit.*, pp. 64, 68.
Barker, *op. cit.*, 1919, II, 416–417 (letter from James Beard to Stephen F. Austin).

121. Mrs. Holley's list does not correspond with Austin's original list.

Mrs. Holley's List	Austin's List as Taken From Names Appearing in his Journal	List of *Lively* Passengers by W. S. Lewis
William Little	Wm. Wilson, from District of Columbia & a late Lt. U. S. Army	James Beard
		Lovelaces
Marshall	James Beard, saddler from St. Louis	Wilson
Edward Lovelace	Doctor Hewitson	O'Neal
Henry Holson	William Little from St. Louis	Stephen Holston
Samuel Fay	Joseph E. Seguin) & other	Phelps, Young
Joseph Polley	Berrimandi) Spaniards met	Harrison
Edward Barr	) & accompanied	Capt. Jennings
Higginbottom	) Austin's party	Capt. Gannon

John Morse	John Lovelace, started, became	Butler
Benjamin Ballou	ill & could not proceed	Lewis
Lt. Barnum	Edward Lovelace	Nelson
Lt. Wilson	Neel	Beddinger
Dr. James Hewetson	Gasper	Williams
	Bellew	Mattigan
and accompanied by	Henry Holsten from Catahoula	Thompson
Seguin	Irwin	Willis
Berrmendi	W. Smithers from Indian (Indiana)	William (servant of
	G. Bush from Natchitoches	Harrison)
	Mr. Barnum, left behind, later	
	joined them	
	Don Erasmo (member of the Spanish	
	party)	
	Marple ⎱	
	Polly ⎰ joined him later	
	Barre	
	Thomas	

REFERENCES:

Eugene C. Barker, "Austin's Journal," *Quarterly of the Texas State Historical Association,* Vol. 286.

Barker, *op. cit.,* 1919, II, II, p. 432–33 (contract with emigrants).

Barker, *op. cit.,* (life of SFA), p. 37–40.

W. S. Lewis, "The Adventures of the Lively Immigrants," *Quarterly of the Texas State Historical Association,* III, p. 1–32.

122. This fairly well follows Austin's own description of the trip. Austin says "Berrimandi." This could well have been Veramendi, Lieutenant Governor of Texas and father-in-law of James Bowie.

123. The group listed by Mrs. Holley were probably the men who had come at Austin's request and built near the ferry at the La Bahia crossing on the Brazos River. The early Anglo corrupted its spelling to Labadie. The crossing was near the old town of Washington. La Bahia was the name of the presidio at Goliad and this would be the road to Goliad rather than San Antonio, which was further north. There were other people present along the Brazos and Colorado before Austin actually began settlement: Brit Bailey, Aylett Buckner, Warran D. C. Hall, Jane Long, and Randall Jones, to name a few.

124. The account of the first trip of the *Lively,* together with the names of the emigrants, was given in great detail by W. S. Lewis, who as a young man was one of the party. (See W. S. Lewis' Note #125.)

125. Both Lewis and Beard stated that the *Lively* arrived first at Galveston in the latter part of December 1821, then reached the mouth of the Brazos in 1822. All of the passengers were unloaded there. It is equally true that Austin did not meet the boat at the mouth of the Colorado where he was supposed to have waited for more than a month. This place was called San Bernardo by the Spaniards, and is where the Colorado River formerly emptied into present Matagorda Bay, then known as Lago de San Bernardo (See Note #71). There is no record of an Austin Elliott having been with Stephen F. Austin at the Colorado. There is no explanation why the passengers left the boat at the mouth of the Brazos without obtaining the tools and supplies that were on board for their use. Beard

and Lewis both seemed to blame the captain of the boat for this failure. The Lovelaces were on the boat and were in nominal control. They had previously been to Mexico with Austin on his first exploratory trip and had loaned him money to finance this venture. A letter from Edward Lovelace to Austin indicated that he did not feel that either the Brazos or the Colorado was the logical port for the colony of Texas, but rather Galveston. It is reasonable to assume that he had no intention of going to the Colorado.

W. S. Lewis did not make the first trip up the river with the others but remained at the mouth of the river where he was finally joined by the returning party. The whole group (with others who had shown up along the coast) then continued up the river to what is known as Fort Bend, the present site of the city of Richmond.

REFERENCES:

Lester G. Bugbee, "What Happened to the Lively," *Quarterly of the Texas State Historical Association,* III, p. 141–48.
Barker, *op. cit.,* 1919, I, 526 (letter from Lovelace to Stephen F. Austin).

126. It is true that Austin went to Mexico without knowing the fate of the *Lively.*

REFERENCE:

Barker, *op. cit.,* p. 39.

127. The poor operation of the *Lively* was probably due to a combination of inexperienced leaders and inadequate preparation. The harbor at the mouth of the Brazos was dangerous, to say the least, and an entrance to Matagorda Bay involved the navigation of Pass Cavallo, which even today is not considered a safe harbor. From there, it is a distance of some thirty miles up the bay to the mouth of the Colorado and then it was necessary to lighter the passengers and products across the bar or delta which had been built by the river. Likewise, the Colorado was on the edge of Austin's early settlement and at the same time was in the area most thickly inhabited by the Karankawa Indians. When the *Lively* party arrived in Texas, Jane Long was still keeping her lonely vigil on Bolivar Peninsula, stubbornly awaiting the return of her husband James Long, who was at this time either in Goliad, or on his way to Mexico City. The *Lively* emigrants thought they saw a pirate ship, but the most famous of the pirates (the Lafitte brothers), had abandoned Galveston some months before and burned most of the improvements they had constructed. Needless to say, the lives of the Lafitte brothers, Jean and Pierre, have been the subject of numerous articles, books, and biographies, and they really have little to do with this publication.

There is no evidence that the *Lively* passengers had any trouble with the Karankawas or any other Indians in the Brazos-Galveston area, nor did Jane Long. Any trouble that the passengers from the *Lively* or *Only Son* (Hawkins' other boat) had was at the mouth of the Colorado, or the port of San Bernardo.

REFERENCES:

Noah Smithwick, *Evolution of a State,* pp. 12–15.
J. H. Kuykendall, "Recollection of Judge Thomas M. Duke," *Quarterly of the Texas State Historical Association,* VI, pp. 247–53.
Papers of Nathaniel Mitchell in possession of J. P. Bryan.
Wharton, *op. cit.,* p. 5.
Sowell, *op. cit.,* pp. 23–46.

128. There were probably other hurricanes that struck the coast of Texas from 1812 to 1837. There is little information about the 1812 storm other than that its destruction was noted as it passed Jamaica and New Orleans. At this time, there were no inhabitants along

the Coast of Texas other than a few scattered Indian tribes. Noah Smithwick mentions in his history of Texas that in 1828 when he went to the Gulf Prairie to help the "McNeel boys" build a cotton gin, they got the necessary iron off the wreck of a schooner found near the house. The 1837 storm was called the "Racer," because it was first sighted by the *HMS Racer* off the Coast of Haiti. It apparently was of great proportions, as it caused tremendous destruction from the tip of Texas to New England. It struck Texas on September 26, 1837, and did not move out to sea, off New York, until the sixth of October.

REFERENCES:

Smithwick, *op. cit.,* p. 28.
Samuel Wood Geiser, "Racer's Storm (1837)," *Field & Laboratory,* pp. 59–67.
Ivan Ray Tannehill, *Hurricanes: Their History and Nature,* p. 230.

129. The reference that the *Lively* was lost on its third trip is true. This was the conclusion of the early University of Texas historian Lester Bugbee. He had a good bit of information about the *Lively* which had not been published before, and, since his article, other information is now available; nevertheless, it is still difficult to ascertain just what did happen to the *Lively,* with regard to its final destination on its first two trips. Some historians had thought it was lost on its first trip (H. Yoakum, *History of Texas, I,* pp. 212–213). Thomas Duke was a passenger on the *Lively* when it was shipwrecked on Galveston Island during the summer of 1822. The fact that the boat made two trips before it was wrecked might explain why some of the articles that evidently were on the boat during its first trip were finally delivered to someone on the Colorado and made their way to San Antonio. The following is a quote from a letter from J. E. B. Austin to Stephen F. Austin, May 4, 1823:

"P.S.—L. Hawkins has left this for the U. S. most of the articles that he sent out in the Lively the first voyage are disposed of in various ways, you will have to settle with him when you return, if you can."

(See *The Austin Papers* Vol. II, letter from Austin to J. E. B. Austin, letter from John Hawkins to Austin, letter from Joseph Hawkins to Austin, and letter from Dr. Sibley to J. E. B. Austin.

Regardless of the success of the first trip made by the *Lively* at least three of the original members of the party and another who joined them at the mouth of the river, stayed in Texas and obtained original grants from Stephen F. Austin, and were among those usually referred to as the "Original Three Hundred." James Beard's league was located in Fort Bend County, and he had descendants there as late as 1939. Another member of the *Lively* party who received a grant in Fort Bend County was William Little. His family played an important part in the beginning of the famous Jaybird-Peckerwood War in Fort Bend County, and particularly the Terry-Gibson Feud. (See Clarence Wharton's *History of Fort Bend County,* Chapter 12, and Sonnichsen's *I'd Rather Die Than Run.*) James Nelson obtained his grant on the Colorado River, and William Morton, who joined the *Lively* party at the mouth of the Brazos, received one league and a half in Fort Bend County. W. S. Lewis remembers Morton as being a brick mason, and if the tradition regarding the Morton Cemetery near Richmond is true, then the restored monument which he built there in 1825 to mark the grave of a man named Robert Gillespie (who was a Mason), is probably the oldest thing remaining that was constructed by one of Austin's colonists in the original colony.

REFERENCES:

Lee, *op. cit.,* p. 167 (reference to Littleberry Hawkins).

Manifests of the *Lively,* November 27, 1821; March 1, 1822 (MSS., National Archives).

Lester G. Bugbee, "The Old Three Hundred," *Quarterly of the Texas State Historical Association,* I, pp. 108–17.

Land Titles, *Texas General Land Office,* 24th of May, 1838.

130. We can assume that this was Sterling McNeel, the bachelor son of John G. McNeel. The following is the heirship excerpt of the McNeel family quoted from the Affidavit of J. H. Shapard, dated February 25, 1890, filed September 18, 1907, at 1 P.M. (recorded in Deed Book 76 of the Deed Records of Brazoria County, Texas):

"Brief of Title to the McNeel Lands. In Brazoria County and affidavit of Heirship.

"John McNeel the founder of the family, died intestate leaving seven children, to-wit: L. H. McNeel; Sterling McNeel; John G. McNeel; P. D. McNeel; Nancy Randon and Elizabeth McNeel; Geo. W. McNeel, another son had died before his father. Elizabeth McNeel also died intestate and her portion vested in the remaining heirs.

"Nancy Randon and her husband conveyed all their interest in the entire estate to her four brothers: See Book 'D' Page 324.

"The following tracts were acquired by the McNeels from the Mexican Government; to-wit:

By John McNeel	One league on the Bernard and one labor on the Brazos.
By Sterling McNeel	One league on the Bernard.
By P. D. McNeel	One league.
By J. G. & G. W. McNeel	One league, one half on the Brazos and one half on the Bernard.
By Geo. W. McNeel	One half league in two tracts on the Bernard.

Besides the land obtained from the Government, by the four brothers in common, the D. G. Mills 155 acres, by deed from D. G. Mills Book 'E' page 344, and 640 acres. . . ."

Sterling was the most prominent of all the McNeel sons. He had two large plantations in Brazoria County. Ann Raney Thomas, in her unpublished memoirs, writes in some detail about her courtship by Sterling McNeel. He was also vividly described by Rutherford B. Hayes, in 1848, when he visited the Peach Point home of Guy M. Bryan, his classmate at Kenyon College:

"Tuesday, January 30—Ride with Mr. Perry over to Sterling McNeal's plantation. A shrewd, intelligent, cynical old bachelor, full of 'wise saws and modern instances;' very fond of telling his own experience and talking of his own affairs. Living alone he has come to think he is the 'be all' and 'end all' here. The haughty and imperious part of a man develops rapidly on one of these lonely sugar plantations, where the owner rarely meets with any except his slaves and minions." (Abigail Curlee, "The History of a Texas Slave Plantation 1831–63," *The Southwestern Historical Quarterly,* XXVI, 113.)

REFERENCES:

Johnson, Malone, *op. cit.,* IV, p. 446–51.

131. William H. Wharton was definitely one of the most influential men during the time that Texas and Coahuila were states and in the early period of the Republic. He lived in Texas for no more than ten years, but his influence was far reaching. From an old but impoverished family in Nashville, Tennessee, he was an attorney and had studied under Dr. Horace Holley (Mrs. Holley's husband), at Transylvania College in Kentucky. He had a brother, John A. Wharton, who also came to Texas and practiced law at Brazoria and who likewise was an early leader in the affairs of Texas. Before settling in Texas, William H. Wharton had shown that he had wonderful judgment and impeccable taste. While residing in Tennessee, he met and married Sarah Ann Groce, the beautiful and only daughter of the richest man in Texas, Jared E. Groce. William H. Wharton settled permanently with his wife at their Eagle Island home (See Sketches #15 and 16) probably in 1829, and from

that time forward began to take an active part in the political activities of the colony. It was not long before he was recognized as the leader of the so-called War Party, which generally opposed anything or anybody connected with the Mexican Government; and it would naturally follow that he would clash with Stephen F. Austin and many of the early settlers, including his father-in-law, who were conservative and, under Austin's leadership, dedicated to a policy of attempting to remain friendly with both the State and National Governments of Mexico. William Wharton took an active part in the Battle of Velasco, was a leader at both the Conventions of 1832 and 1833, and at most of the meetings leading up to the Consultation of 1835. Branch T. Archer, Stephen F. Austin, and William H. Wharton were selected at the Consultation of 1835 as Commissioners to the United States to raise funds for the Republic. It was during this time that he and Stephen F. Austin reconciled their problems and, evidently, became good friends, as Wharton encouraged Austin to run for President of the Republic. Wharton was elected senator from Brazoria to the first Congress and was then appointed Minister to the United States in 1836, and obtained recognition of the Republic by the United States. He was elected senator from Brazoria County again, but accidentally shot himself in March of 1839 at the home of his deceased brother-in-law, Jared E. Groce, Jr. He lived but a few days after the accident and died at the home of another brother-in-law, Leonard W. Groce. His body was carried to Eagle Island where he was buried in the Wharton family cemetery.

REFERENCES:

Sarah Wharton Groce Berlet, "Autobiography of a Spoon," 1828–1956 (unpublished copy of MS. in possession of Mrs. Adele Caldwell of Freeport, Texas).

Laura Hale, "The Groces and Whartons in Early History" (Master's Thesis, University of Texas, 1942).

Sarah Groce Berlet, "The Groce Book" (unpublished MS. in possession of Sarah Groce Berlet).

Rosa Groce Berlet, "Jared Ellison Groce," *Southwestern Historical Quarterly,* XX, pp. 358–68.

Clarence R. Wharton, The Whartons of Old Brazoria (unpublished copy of MS. in the J. P. Bryan Collection).

132. Actually, most of the peach loam is light and has a distinct reddish tone. A quick trip through Clement's Prison Farm on Highway 36 during the spring will give a good picture of what this property looked like. There is no question that it was very fertile and, because of the loam characteristics, easy to work.

133. Indications are that most of the planters along the lower Brazos were considerate of their slaves, if such an expression could be used at this time.

REFERENCES:

Abigail Curlee, "The History of a Texas Slave Plantation, 1831–63," *Southwestern Historical Quarterly,* XXVI, pp. 79–127.

Abigail Curlee, "A Study of Texas Slave Plantations, 1822–1865," (Doctor's Thesis, University of Texas, 1932).

134. Stephen F. Austin died at Columbia on December 27, 1836, of pneumonia. At that time he was Secretary of State and was making a strenuous effort to obtain recognition of the Republic of Texas by the United States. His body was carried to Perry's Landing on the steamship *Yellowstone* and he was buried in the family cemetery at Peach Point. His remains were moved to the State Cemetery in Austin in 1910. A tomb still marks his

burial place in the Peach Point Cemetery.

Descendants of Emily Margaret Austin have been buried in the cemetery, a short distance from the original home, since 1833, when her infant daughter, Mary Bryan, was buried there. The cemetery is known as Gulf Prairie Cemetery, the Gulf Prairie Presbyterian Cemetery, or the Peach Point Cemetery. Regardless of its name, the cemetery and the Gulf Prairie Presbyterian Church are located on a three-acre tract which is a part of the Peach Point homestead. The cemetery is really a cemetery within a cemetery as the Bryan and Perry heirs have, from the beginning, maintained their own burial plots, while the other portions of the cemetery are used for people residing in the area generally known as Gulf Prairie. For many years descendants of Emily Margaret Perry have acted as trustees for the Cemetery Association. At present, these trustees are: S. S. Perry, Jr., and W. Joel Bryan, Jr., the third position having been vacant since the recent death of Henry Austin Bryan.

It was obvious that Mrs. Holley had not forgotten Stephen F. Austin. She was certainly definitely interested in writing Austin's life, and it is strange that, given her general aggressiveness, she did not start the work and then get the necessary information from the Perrys later on. She was a widow and it may well have been that in her circumstances she thought she should have been paid for the job. Guy M. Bryan and Emily Margaret visited Mrs. Holley in Louisville in 1837, but there is no clear record of how the Mary Austin Holley Papers were obtained by Guy M. Bryan, who gave the Austin Papers to the University of Texas.

REFERENCES:

George L. Hammeken, "Memory of Austin Regarding His Death," *Southwestern Historical Quarterly,* XX, pp. 369–80.

Lee, *op. cit.,* pp. 276, 285, 288.

See Notes #60 and #102.

Marguerite Johnson, *Christ Church Cathedral 1839–1964* (Houston: Cathedral Press, 1964), p. 13.

135. A typical colloquialism: People were always going "up country" and "down the river."

136. Evidently, the Dr. Jones referred to was Dr. Levi Jones, who attended Stephen F. Austin at the time of his death in Columbia in 1836. There is no indication that Levi Jones was related to Anson Jones, who was the last President of the Republic of Texas, and also a doctor. (See Note #11 about the killing.)

Most of the music for the various dances was furnished by the slaves.

REFERENCES:

J. P. Bryan, *op. cit.,* I, p. 80.

Nixon, *op. cit.,* p. 183.

137. It is hard to believe that the grass-fed steers were as tender as they appeared to Mrs. Holley.

138. Prairie fires are a normal phenomenon of the Gulf Coast salt grass country. This bunch grass, in the world of botany, is Distichlis Spicata (Variety Spicata is also called Seashore Salt Grass, Variety Distichlis Spicata is also called Inland or Desert Salt Grass and Variety Texana is called Texas Salt Grass); it contains a great deal of oil and will burn even when the roots are wet. In a blowing wind one of these fires can become a roaring holocaust. Ranchers burn the grass frequently, as the new growth is supposed to be beneficial.

139. The following is a quote from T. L. Smith's "Steamboats on the Brazos."

"1. The *Old Columbia*—1830: It was said by one writer that she was the first steamer to travel from New Orleans to Galveston, but another report says that the *Old Columbia* plied up to Washington in 1830 before she was wrecked on a sand bar."

It is hard to believe that the *Columbia* was on the Brazos as early as 1830 because when Henry Austin arrived in 1830 with the *Ariel* he did not feel there was enough commerce to justify a shipping business. See Note #13 for reference to the first steamboats on the Brazos.)

140. The Westall family was prominent in the early history of the county, Thomas Westall having been one of Austin's original three hundred. Although he was granted property in other parts of the colony, his home tract was in Brazoria County, adjoining the Greenville McNeel plantation. Since Thomas Westall, the founder of the family, was dead by January 14, 1835, it is difficult to ascertain who the Westalls are that are mentioned by Mrs. Holley.

Eliza Westall married J. E. B. Austin, who was Stephen F. Austin's younger brother, and they had a child who was named for his uncle. A provision in Austin's will regarding the estate of this young man, who died before reaching twenty-one, resulted in a bitter lawsuit between the mother and Emily Margaret Perry. After J. E. B. Austin died, Eliza had married Zeno Phillips and then, on February 25, 1836, William G. Hill.

REFERENCE:

Thomas W. Streeter, *Bibliography of Texas 1795–1845,* II, p. 494 (record of case: Eliza M. Westall and William G. Hill vs. James F. Perry and wife).

141. The heirs of Major James P. Caldwell still own a large portion of their original plantation, which joined Peach Point. Major Caldwell was active in the early affairs of Texas and was one of the participants of the Battle of Velasco. John Caldwell, a great grandson, resides on the plantation.

142. The Widow Munson was Ann Bynum Pierce Munson, who had first married Henry Munson, who died in the cholera epidemic. (Note James F. Perry's letter to Stephen F. Austin, *The Austin Papers,* II, p. 1010.) Henry Munson was one of the first persons to be buried at Peach Point. Ann Bynum Pierce Munson Caldwell had five children when married to Henry Munson, and two during her marriage to James P. Caldwell. The Munson family moved from the Gulf Prairie area to Bailey's Prairie, and opened a plantation there on the Smith and Bailey Leagues, Abstracts #129 and #38, respectively. The widow Munson has as many heirs living in and around Brazoria County as does the widow Bryan (Emily Margaret Austin Bryan Perry). From the beginning, the Munson family has been prominent in affairs of the county and State. M. S. Munson served as District Judge of the 23rd Judicial District for more than thirty-one years and was never opposed for the office.

REFERENCE:

Affidavit of Heirship of Henry Munson and Wife, Vol. 50, p. 569, Deed Records of Brazoria County, Texas.

143. William Joel Bryan (Emily Margaret's oldest son who was born in Herculaneum, Missouri, on December 14, 1815), came to Texas with his mother and stepfather, James F. Perry, in 1831. Joel Bryan was at the Battle of Bexar, but he caught measles and was unable to take part in the Battle of San Jacinto.

The town of Bryan, Texas, is named for him, but he resided at his plantation known as Durazno (which is Spanish for peach), located on part of the premium land which Mrs.

Holley thought should have been hers. He died there in 1903 at the age of eighty-seven. Some of his heirs still own a portion of his original plantation: Mrs. Alvah C. Learned, Dr. Everett B. Lewis of Houston, and Mr. Thomas Lewis of Galveston County. (Mr. and Mrs. A. Learned have a home on the property.)

W. Joel Bryan left five hundred acres of the Durazno plantation, upon which were located the principal improvements, to his son, Samuel Irvin Bryan. Samuel divided the tract equally between his daughter, Louella Bryan Burrus, and his nephew, Samuel Irvin Stratton. The tract that Mrs. Burrus received is now owned by the Learneds and Lewises. The other tract is now owned by Mrs. R. E. L. Stringfellow of Freeport, Texas. The present house, on the tract owned by Mrs. Stringfellow, includes a small portion of the W. Joel Bryan original plantation home.

REFERENCES:

Memoirs of Guy M. Bryan.
Mrs. Guy (Lois Brock) Adriance & Mrs. John (Adele Perry) Caldwell, *loc. cit.*

144. An interesting event in connection with the Perry home during the war is revealed by the letter that James F. Perry wrote in Galveston on April 26, 1836, to his wife Emily Margaret, who was in the "runaway scrape," the flight of the inhabitants before the advancing Mexican forces. He had been in Galveston with the group, under Colonel James Morgan, which was attempting to fortify the east end of the island. James F. Perry and Captain Fuller had been sent, by Colonel Morgan, to Velasco to get some tools. James F. Perry went on from Velasco to Peach Point where he found everything in good order, nothing having been disturbed by the Mexican Army. General Urrea, who was in command of the army, did not get any closer to the coast than Brazoria. Perry was able to bring back from the plantation a good many things which he intended to ship to New Orleans. Although the letter is dated April 26, he did not then know that the Battle of San Jacinto had been fought.

REFERENCES:

The Perry-Bryan Papers (Archives) The University of Texas Library.
Carlos E. Castaneda, *The Mexican Side of the Texan Revolution* (Dallas: P. L. Turner Company, 1956), pp. 242–43.

145. Mrs. Holley was right about the value of the land for grazing purposes, as it has supported several large ranch operations including an extensive one carried on by the Bryan brothers, sons of William Joel Bryan, and later by Mr. R. E. L. Stringfellow of Freeport, Texas. Even more important was her conclusion regarding the Mound. This was a salt dome known as Bryan Mound, and for many years the Freeport Sulphur Company conducted a sulphur-mining operation on the property, producing more than five million tons of sulphur.

Since the early 1940s, the Dow Chemical Company has conducted salt-mining operations on the property and has produced infinite tons of brine for its integrated chemical operations at Freeport. At the present time, Humble Oil and Refining Company is carrying on exploratory operations for oil and gas. Heirs of W. Joel Bryan still own extensive acreage surrounding the salt dome.

146. It is possible that Mrs. Holley saw many of the famous whooping cranes, which are now almost extinct.

147. The general terrain of the country described by Mrs. Holley is much the same, but there have been definite artificial changes, such as the diversion of the Brazos River to enter the Gulf at the point almost where Mrs. Holley and Emily Margaret Perry probably ar-

rived at the beach. Also, the Intracoastal Waterway has been dredged parallel to the Gulf. Thus, it is no longer possible to ride from Peach Point to the beach, or Bryan Mound, without crossing several bridges.

148. Mrs. Holley had an opportunity to meet both the famous partners of the firm Williams & McKinney. Samuel May Williams became Stephen F. Austin's secretary at an early date and they were closely associated for many years. Most of the Mexican Grants in the Texas Land Office were written in his fine hand. Shortly before the Revolution, Williams became deeply involved in the land speculation in the then Capital of Texas and Coahuila (Monclovia), and Austin and Williams' relationship became strained. Regardless of what the general public may have thought of Samuel May Williams and Thomas F. McKinney, their firm was responsible for a major part of the financing of the Texas Revolution, and theirs was the leading financial institution in the Republic and State of Texas for many years. After the Revolution, they moved their business offices to Galveston.

It is interesting to note Williams' attitude about Austin, as Stephen F. Austin was outspoken in his criticism of his former secretary; however, it is apparent that he had a great deal of respect for Williams even to the end.

Mrs. McKinney, prior to her marriage, lived in Nacogdoches and was named Nancy Wilson, and Mrs. Williams was Sarah Scott, formerly of Kentucky.

REFERENCES:

Barker, *op. cit.*, III, p. 424 (letter from Williams to Austin, August 29, 1836).
Ibid., p. 446 (letter from Austin to Williams, November 13, 1836).

149. It was many years before Mr. Williams succeeded in establishing the first bank in Texas. Williams secured a charter from the State of Coahuila and Texas on April 30, 1835, to open the Commercial & Agricultural Bank at Galveston, but it was December 30, 1847, before the bank was finally opened.

REFERENCE:

Johnson, Malone, *op. cit.*, X., pp. 289–90.

150. Almost any plant or vegetable can be grown on the sand ridges within a stone's throw of the Gulf if partially protected from the salt spray.

151. "The Open Sea," a poem by Mary Austin Holley, was published in the *San Luis Advocate*, April 13, 1841.

152. Equally surprising is the fact that the Gulf Coast, now as then, has an abundance of wild life, particularly deer. There are large herds of these animals still on many of the lower islands, and the Powderhorn Ranch (near the old town of Indianola) has a game preserve which is one of the principal sources of deer trapped for restocking other areas of the State.

153. Veslaco and Quintana at this time were important towns in Texas. Most of the shipping was through the Brazos River and a continuous fight was going on between the two towns for the location of the Customs House and other governmental buildings. At this date, neither Galveston nor Houston had been established as ports.

The Archer House was named for Branch T. Archer, who, with Stephen F. Austin and William H. Wharton, was selected commissioner from Texas, at the beginning of the Revolution to acquire funds in the United States. Archer was born in Virginia in 1790. He practiced medicine there, and served two terms in the House of Burgesses before coming to Texas. From the beginning, he was one of the leaders of the so-called War Party. Archer had a grant of land along Oyster Creek (Branch T. Archer League, Abstract #9, Deed Records of Brazoria County, Texas), but indications are that he spent most of his time at the home of William H. Wharton and supposedly is buried in the Wharton Cemetery at Eagle Island. (See Sketches #15 and #16). The following is the impression that Branch T. Archer made on one person in New Orleans, January 1, 1836:

"The Commissioners from Texas, Gen'l Stephen F. Austin, Hon'l Branch T. Archer, and Hon'l Wm. H. Wharton, and several other Texans, have arrived this morning in five days from Brazoria, by water. Introduced to Austin and Archer, who both board here. Wharton does not stop here. They bring particulars of the capture of San Antonio, and are in high spirits about Texas. Archer is particularly excited and vehement. He talks too much and too loud. Austin is more prudent. He appears to be a sensible and unpretending business man. This house is much thronged, many persons are crowding to the bar room to see the Commissioners and hear about Texas. Indeed, we can scarcely hear of anything else. Spent most of the day in conversing with them, and in listening to conversations about that country, its character, condition and prospects." (Diary of Fairfax Gray, page 64.)

REFERENCES:

D. W. C. Baker, *A Texas Scrapbook* (life of Dr. Branch T. Archer by Barker) (New York: A. S. Barnes & Co., 1875), p. 265.

J. P. Bryan, *op. cit.*, I, pp. 22–26 (customs at Galveston & Quintana).

Forrest E. Ward, "The Lower Brazos Region of Texas," Chapter XI: The Port of Velasco, (Doctor's Thesis, University of Texas, January, 1962).

Wharton I. Green, *Recollections and Reflections* (Edwards & Broughton Printing Company, 1906).

L. W. Kemp & Lewis J. Wilson Correspondence, (J. P. Bryan Collection).

154. General Thomas J. Green was, to say the least, the moving spirit of Velasco. He appeared in Velasco just in time to keep the *Invincible* from sailing to Vera Cruz with Santa Anna. He was one of the organizers of the Velasco Association, which laid out the old town of Velasco. It would be too much to list all the accomplishments of this famous man. He wrote a book about his experiences in the Mier Expedition, *Journal of the Texian Expedition Against Mier,* published in 1835, and his son Wharton Green also wrote a book, *Recollections and Reflections* (published in 1906), which contains a good deal of information about his father. The General was a racing enthusiast and his horses were frequently listed in the racing journal. The following is quoted from *Spirit of the Times*, April 4, 1840 (a national publication).

"Winning horses in 1839 at *two mile heats:*

'Coloradian' [Colorado?] owned by Gen. Thomas J. Green, prize 250 p., wt. 73 lb., beat 'Milam' at Houston, Texas, on April 17, 1839. 'Coloradian' is listed as a 3 year old.

'Colorado' owned by General Thomas J. Green, 3 years old, (prize 400 p, wt. 83. Beat 'Kleber' in the time of 3:55–3:56 at Velasco, Texas on April 30, 1839.

'Colorado' owned by General Thomas J. Green, prize 2900 s.(?), 97 lb. wt., time 4:17–4: 12–4:19, beat 'Sam Houston' at Galveston, Texas, on December 24, 1839."

The general was a convivial person, a fact illustrated by the following letters to Ashbel Smith.

"
                                      Velasco, Feb 17, 1839

My Dear Dr.

Our spring meeting of the Jockey Club commences on the 29th inst—I write for you to come to see us on that occasion—our house is yours—Many fine women & horses are in attendance all ready—Be sure to come. Dr. Archer & myself will be certain to expect you—

                                                Your friend truly
                                              Thos J. Green"

"
                                        Velasco, Feby 19, 1839

[torn] Friend

We shall have one week of raceing and frolic in this town (commencing on the twentieth of next month) and Genl Green, and myself are keeping *first* rate, bachelors quarters. Enough to say, we shall be extremely happy to have you with us, during the sports of the week. You shall have a bed, a plate, and a stall for the horse—which is enough for a bachelor. Though, if we have other comforts, you shall divide equally

I will assure you a display of fashion and beauty; you may find a wife among our girls

Respectfully your Friend & Svt
B. T. Archer"

REFERENCE:

Ashbel Smith Collection, University of Texas Archives.

155. Mrs. Holley had seen the fort at Velasco before. (See Note #14 which quotes her first impression.) In 1936, an historical marker was placed at the location of the fort, but there is no evidence at this time of any graves. An estimated seven Texans and forty-two Mexicans were killed in the Battle of Velasco.

REFERENCES:

Brown, *op. cit.,* I, pp. 182–88.

Charles Adams Gulick, Jr., Katherine Elliott, eds., *The Papers of Mirabeau Buonaparte Lamar* (Battle of Velasco). Austin: Von Boeckman-Jones, 1921–27, I, pp. 132–36.

J. P. Bryan, *loc. cit.,* III (notes on Battle of Velasco.)

156. Refer to Sketch #3 on Quintana.

157. Lead water, a dilute solution of basic lead acetate, used as an external application, especially in cases of sprains or bruises.

158. The William H. Jack plantation was located approximately eight miles from the mouth of the river on a five-hundred-acre tract in the Stephen F. Austin 5-League Grant, Abstract #19, and directly across from Perry's Landing.

There were a number of Jack brothers in Texas during the colonial period; William H. and Patrick C. Jack being the most prominent of at least six brothers. Mrs. Holley does not give a description of the house, nor did she sketch it; however there must have been substantial improvements there at this early date. The main dwelling, which was close to the Brazos River, was a large L-shaped building of a story and a half. Several of the rooms were of solid brick, which was baked on the plantation, and the rooms inside were plastered-over lattice, and there was a large double fireplace. Laurent Cherouze, who was a French citizen, acquired the property in 1851, and it was later purchased by the editor's grandfather, J. P. Bryan, in 1867 after his return from the Civil War. He operated a general merchandise store here for many years, and the editor's father, W. Joel Bryan, was born here in March 1874.

The building was fairly well preserved as late as 1942 when it was sold by William Joel Bryan to the Dow Chemical Company. Today, there is nothing left to commemorate this historical spot, other than a portion of the brick floor. As with many of the other plantations, there is no way of telling when and how the house was built originally, or what was added by subsequent owners. This must certainly have been one of the oldest places along the Brazos. In 1933, the editor interviewed Eliza Harris, who was at least ninety-two years of age at the time. She had been a slave and had lived all her life within a short distance of this property. She stated that the house had been there as long as she could remember.

159. The Calvit home was located at the site of the present town of Clute, Texas, on a

portion of the Jared E. Groce League, which adjoins the Alexander Calvit League, Abstract #49. Mr. Calvit's wife was a sister of Jane Wilkinson Long. Alexander Calvit, generally known as "Sandy," was a good friend of Austin's for some time, and family tradition has it that Mrs. Long and Mrs. Calvit made the black buckskin suit that Austin wore in several of his portraits (see Austin miniature on ivory painted in Mexico City). By the time Austin had become a prisoner in Mexico City Calvit had definitely broken with him, and he wrote a letter requesting that the Mexicans retain Austin forever.

REFERENCES:

Barker, *op. cit.,* p. 391.
Guy M. Bryan Letter to Mrs. S. M. W. Compton, August 20, 1891.

160. The location of the homesite of the Crosbys was referred to previously in Note #48.

161. The fate of the various Mexican prisoners was certainly a sorry one. It seems that these poor unfortunates were picked up and scattered throughout the colonies as servants. What would have happened had this been the final fate of the members of, say, the Mier Expedition?

REFERENCES:

"Colonel Amasa Turner's Reminiscences of Galveston," III, p. 46; and "The Reminiscences of Mrs. Dilue Harris," *Quarterly of the Texas State Historical Association*: IV, p. 178.

162. It would be interesting to know which McNeel home Mrs. Holley was describing in 1838. The McNeels had plantations in the area known as Ellersly, Lowwood, and Pleasant Grove, as well as the Pleasant McNeel plantation. The beautiful home built by Greenville McNeel, known as Ellersly, was generally recognized as the most elegant home in Austin's colony. The following is a description of the house by an early visitor:

"Ellersley plantation, the home of J. Greenville McNeel, was a large two-story brick house of 21 rooms—faced west and had galleries west and south the entire length of the house, supported by immense pillars. It had marble hearths and mantels. The ceilings in the various rooms and halls were beautifully decorated. The furniture was of the handsomest—being very heavy, and of mahogany and walnut. All the rooms were carpeted. It was considered, in its day, the finest home in Texas." (*The Old Plantations and Their Owners of Brazoria County, Texas* by Abner J. Strobel, 25–26.)

This beautiful home burned about 1900; however, the overseer's home and some of the slave quarters are in good repair since they were built of brick.

Greenville McNeel married Ann A. Westall. (See Note #140.)

Lowwood was the plantation home of Robert Mills, who married Elizabeth McNeel. (See previous Notes # 20, 52, and references.)

None of the McNeel family own any of the original property granted to them in Brazoria County; however, a descendant of the McNeel family (John Perry McNeel), lives in West Columbia, Texas.

163. There remain three hundred acres of the original Westall plantation, which are owned by Evan Shelby Smith and E. Gertrude Smith of San Antonio, Texas, the father and aunt of Mrs. Josephine S. Masterson and Gretchen S. Bryan of Houston. None of the original improvements are intact. There is an indication of the original cemetery where John Austin, among others, may have been buried.

164. Mrs. Holley raises an interesting question regarding travel from Galveston to Matagorda on the beach. It is possible that there was ferry service across all the numerous streams

at various times during the early history of Brazoria County. William Bollaert described a trip that he made from Galveston to Matagorda in 1842. A ferry was maintained by the Ducroz family near the mouth of the Bernard River at the time of Mrs. Holley's visit. (Descendants of this family still live in Brazoria County and own property along the beach west of the San Bernard.) Also, there was a ferry at one time across Cold Pass and probably, spasmodically, across San Luis Pass to join with Galveston Island. It is certainly impossible to make the trip now.

REFERENCES:

William Bollaert, *William Bollaert's Texas,* W. Eugene Hollon & Ruth Lapham Butler, eds. (Norman: University of Oklahoma Press, 1956), pp. 84–88.
Refer to Note #147.

165. E and H were Emily and Henrietta, Mrs. Holley's nieces, Joel would be Joel Bryan, and Dr. Jones would be Dr. Levi Jones. We can assume that the young men were courting.

166. It is a shame that Mrs. Holley did not write a later book about Texas when she had become really familiar with the Republic. It appears that she has again lost interest in the promised land.

167. Charles Austin was Mary Austin Holley's brother, who was an ordained Episcopal minister in Maryland. He was also the one to whom the letters were addressed in her first book. William Brand was her son-in-law.

REFERENCES:

Lee, *loc. cit.* (for more information about brother Charles).

168. As previously noted, Mrs. Holley arrived at Quintana and Velasco when the two towns were at their peak during the early period of the Texas Republic. Later visitors, particularly Francis Sheridan (a member of the British Diplomatic Corps), did not appreciate their elegance. The following is quoted from *Galveston Island: The Journal of Francis Sheridan, 1839–1840:*

"Velasco is by no means a gigantic town, as it numbers no more than between 20 and 30 irregularly built huts and houses. Nor does it afford much gratification to a lover of Picturesque situated as it is on a low sandy beach which soon merges into a flat shrubless, prairie extending as far as the eye can reach. There are a few houses on the left side of the river, one of which is tenanted by no less a person than my friend Thomson, but the greatest part locate on the right. Green's dwelling being by far the best. No church as yet 'with silent finger points to heaven' and the good Christians of the place are content to offer up occasional devotions in each others houses. As some sort of recompence there is a Court House, on the top of which floated the Yankee Colors as well as those of Texas. In front of this is 'the Battery' as they think fit to term it, consisting of an old brass 18 pounder with a touch-hole equivalent in circumference to the mouth of Mrs. Sharp. . . ."

169. We would assume that Mrs. Holley is referring to Judge Benjamin C. Franklin, who evidently tried the only case in Texas during the period of the provisional and interim governments:

"On March 12, 1836, President ad interim of the Republic of Texas, by ordinance created a Special District Court for Brazoria County to try the case of the Brig Pocket, which had been seized by the Invincible of the Texas Navy for attempting to carry contraband goods to Mexico, and appointed James Collingsworth Special District Judge to hold said Court. Collingsworth declining to serve, and thereupon President Burnet appointed Benjamin C. Franklin Judge of said Court The case was tried before Judge Franklin and the vessel condemned, and that Court was the first District Court held in the Republic of Texas. Although Judge Franklin appears to have been appointed for the special purpose of trying the case of Brig Pocket, he continued to act generally as such District Judge until he became the first District Judge for Brazoria County under the Acts of the First Congress of the Republic of Texas passed at Columbia. The first term of the District Court of Brazoria County created by the Acts of the First Congress commenced on March 29 (see), 1837." (Papers of Lewis J. Wilson.)

Miss McConnell could possibly be the daughter of Daniel B. McConnell, who was a resident of Brazoria County at this time.

REFERENCES:

District Court Records of Brazoria County, Texas: Trial of Brig Pocket.
L. W. Kemp's Notes on the Holley Diary, Mary Austin Holley Collection, University of Texas Archives.

170. More indications of Mrs. Holley's various talents. She sketched, spoke at least two foreign languages—Spanish and French—had her favorite guitar with her most of the time, wrote poems, composed lyrics, and played the piano and harp.

171. Sarah A. Groce was the daughter of Jared E. Groce and Mary A. Waller, and was born in Lincoln County, Georgia, in 1810. She was educated in both Nashville, Tennessee, and New York. It is not certain that she came to Texas with her father in 1822; however, she did return to Texas in 1827 and a short time thereafter married William H. Wharton, whom she had met while she was in Tennessee. Her father gave the Whartons the land upon which the Eagle Island plantation was developed, and built their home. They had one son, John A. Wharton, who was a Confederate general (Terry's Texas Rangers). He was killed almost immediately after the war by one of his officers. He had previously married Penelope Johnson, the daughter of the Governor of South Carolina, and they had one child, Katherine. Sarah A. Groce outlived both her daughter-in-law and her granddaughter, and when she died in 1879 practically all of the estate that had been owned by her family had been dissipated.

REFERENCE:

See Note #131 and Sketches 15 and 16.

172. The Mr. and Mrs. Waller referred to would be Edwin Waller and his wife, who was Julia M. DeShield. Edwin Waller, as well as Wharton, Green, Archer, and others, was one of the moving spirits in the development of Velasco. He was, likewise, an important figure in many Texas affairs for a number of years, among other things being the first mayor of Austin. His grandson, Edwin Waller, was distinguished as being the last mayor of Quintana. Having been elected the first mayor of Quintana, Waller served for several years in this capacity, also being postmaster and the operator of a general store. The town did not prosper after its incorporation and the most accurate description would be that it was abandoned. Nothing was done about the city government and we can assume that Edwin Waller remained at the head of the defunct government. He later moved to San Marcos where his political fate took a turn for the worse, as he was mentioned many years later in Ripley's "Believe It or Not" as a man who ran for eighteen elective offices and was defeated on each occasion.

The Wallers and the Whartons were related.

REFERENCES:

Memoirs of Follet Shannon, 1958, MS., J. P. Bryan Collection.
"Reminiscences of Judge Edwin Waller," *op. cit.*, IV, pp. 33–53 (author's notes by P. E. Phareson).

Minutes of the Commissioners Court of Brazoria County, Texas, 1891.

173. The tradition of the Wharton live oak is certainly unusual. Records indicate that the largest oak tree in Texas (near Rockport), is about 35 feet in circumference. The famous cypress or ahuehuete tree at Santa Maria del Tule on the road from Oaxaca to Mitla in Mexico (still considered the largest living thing in the world) is now supposed to be 162 feet, and is even larger in circumference than the famous sequoia trees in California. No record of a tree the size referred to by Mrs. Holley has been found in Brazoria County, as far as the editor can ascertain.

174. The largest topaz in the world is on display at the New York Museum of Natural History and weighs over 600 pounds. (See the illustration of a Spanish stirrup, which would have been very much like the one owned by Wharton.) None of these articles mentioned by Mrs. Holley has been preserved.

General Castrillon was one of the participants in the Battle of San Jacinto, and an account of his death can be found in *Day of San Jacinto* by Frank X. Tolbert.

175. Mrs. Long was Jane Wilkinson Long, who is mentioned in Notes #127 and 159. Dr. Jones was Dr. Levi Jones referred to in Notes #136 and 165. Dr. Charman might be W. J. Chatham of Harrison County. Dr. Stone might be Alexander Stone of Limestone County. Dr. Jackson might be A. W. Jackson of Harrison County.

REFERENCES:

Nixon, *op. cit.*, p. 473.
L. W. Kemp's Notes on the Holley Diary, University of Texas Archives.

176. William B. Scates was born in Fairfax, Virginia, in 1802. He arrived in Texas in 1831. He took part in the Siege of Bexar, fought in the Battle of San Jacinto, and was a signer of the Declaration of Independence. At the age of sixty-two, he joined the Confederate Army and died in 1882 in Colorado County.

177. Mrs. Blackwell was probably the wife of Thomas Blackwell, who was elected District Clerk of Brazoria County on January 8, 1838.

REFERENCE:

Election Return Records of Brazoria County, Texas.

178. All through the coastal area of Texas are the islands of trees. This was noted by many early travelers.

179. Mrs. Holley was carrying on a rather dangerous operation to say the least. These prairie fires can be deadly and frequently the smoke is almost as bad as the flames.

180. To make excellent bread?

181. The Bates family lived in and near the town of Brazoria at an early time, but there is no information regarding the family during Mrs. Holley's visit.

REFERENCE:

Affidavits of Bates Heirship, Vol. 76, p. 90, Deed Records of Brazoria County, Texas (two affidavits: W. Fort Smith & W. H. Sharp).

182. The following is all the information that we have concerning the *Crusader:*
"CRUSADER, steamboat, Mobile, Alabama, 121 tons, Thomas Hereford, Owner and Master. (Ship Registers & Enrollments, Survey of Federal Archives in Louisiana in 1831–1840.) (See also Note #13.)

REFERENCE:

New Orleans Ship Registrations, 1810–1824, W. P. A. (Typescript, University of Texas Archives).

183. Mrs. Holley still seems to be interested in agreeable gentlemen.

184. Although there were at this time tentative plans for a railroad between the two settlements they never materialized. A railroad was built on the east side of the Brazos to Houston in 1858.

REFERENCE:

Rogers, *loc. cit.*

185. On a good day you can probably still catch the same species of fish in the Brazos River, or Oyster Creek.

186. The book that Mrs. Holley refers to is *Viage a los Estados Unidos del Norte de America,* by D. Lorenzo de Zavala (Paris Imp de Docourchant, 1834). Lorenzo de Zavala was very prominent in the early affairs of the Mexican Republic and at one time was minister to France. Having severed his relations with Santa Anna at an early time, he joined the Texas cause and was elected a vice-president of the interim government. His home was on Buffalo Bayou across from San Jacinto, and he died in an accident soon after the battle.

187. Thomas Chalmers, *"A Series of Discourses on the Christian Revelation, Viewed in Connection with the Modern Astronomy,"* ninth edition; Edinburg: 1818.

188. The book mentioned is *The Rambler in Mexico* by Charles Joseph Latrobe; London: R. B. Seeley and W. Burnside, 1836; and, also New York: Harper and Brothers, 1836.

189. And "make a grito" he did—and many more. (Using an idiomatic expression in Spanish resulting from Hidalgo's action in Dolores which initiated the Mexican War of Independence.)

REFERENCE:

See references under Note #28.

190. Joel Bryan seems to be a regular visitor. At this time he was twenty-three years old and we can assume that he was interested in either Emily or Henrietta.

191. Strange to think there would be buffaloes in this area at any time.

192. There were probably many people up and down the banks of the Brazos River and Oyster Creek such as "Old Rock" and his family (See Sketch #6).

193. Evidently there were a good many strangers going and coming in Texas at this time. The New York Directory of April, 1838, page 61, lists:

1835/36 Crook, William T., merchant, 217 Pearl, h. 448 Houston
        Crook & Watt, 217 Pearl (first entry)
        Watt, William, merchant, 217 Pearl (first entry)
1836/37 Crook, William T., merchant, 217 Pearl, h. 448 Houston
        Crook, Watt & Co., importers, 217 Pearl (last entry)
        Watt, William, merchant, 217 Pearl
1837/38 Crook & Co., Wm. T., merchants, 217 Pearl, h. 448 Houston
        Watt, William, merchant, 40 Pine

194. Mrs. Holley shows her proficiency in Spanish.

195. About the only place the anniversary of the Battle of San Jacinto is now celebrated is

at San Jacinto Battlegrounds proper.

196. Navigation probably was fairly simple as far as Bolivar for the shallow-draft steamboats in Mrs. Holley's time.

197. We would suppose that vinegar might have been stored in oak containers.

198. The Galveston Naval Yard was formally established in 1838; however the port facilities were used by the first ships of the Navy of the Republic as early as 1836. The obvious military advantage of Galveston harbor caused it to be used before adequate military installations could be built and the civilian suppliers were forced to accept Republic currency in repayment. More than one merchant's business failed before he could redeem the paper money.

The merchant brig *Potomac* was purchased from L. M. Hitchcock of Galveston in 1837. A grand total of $10,000 was spent to convert her into a ship of war. A Mr. H. Sanderson was the supplier and he went bankrupt after unsuccessfully attempting to collect from the Republic. It developed that the *Potomac* was not seaworthy, and she never left the Galveston Naval Yard but was used as a receiving ship for that station. During the period that Mrs. Holley visited the Naval Yard, the Texas Navy had only the following personnel: two lieutenants, two midshipmen, a doctor, two pursers, and two seamen. The Mr. Wright mentioned was Lt. Frank B. Wright, the highest ranking officer in the Navy. It seems that Houston was on an economy move during this period and the Navy was one of his chief targets. (As a further note the two seamen in the Texas Navy were both deserters from the American Navy.)

REFERENCES:

Jim Dan Hill, *The Texas Navy in Forgotten Battles and Shirtsleeve Diplomacy* (Chicago: The University of Chicago Press, 1937).
Navy Papers, Texas State Archives.

199. The book Mrs. Holley refers to here is *Opinions on Various Subjects Dedicated to the Industrious Producer,* by William McClure (London: 1831).

200. See Note #186 concerning de Zavala.

201. The book mentioned by Mrs. Holley is *Trip to Texas and the West* by Amos Andrew Parker (Concord, New Hampshire: White & Fisher, 1835).

202. This last book referred to by Mrs. Holley, which she intended to purchase, is *Society Manners & Politics in the United States* by Michel Chevalier (third ed.; Paris, 1834).

ACKNOWLEDGMENTS

It would be impossible for the editor to recognize and thank all those—historians, archivists, librarians, secretaries, University of Texas personnel—whose aid has made it possible for him to annotate the Mary Austin Holley Diary. Certain persons, however, should be specifically mentioned.

When the diary was acquired by the University of Texas, the editor was working on a book to be named "Velasco" and had done a great deal of previous research on the history of the area that Mrs. Holley visited. The work on "Velasco" was originally undertaken to complete the extensive research previously done by the late Louis J. Wilson, Brazoria County attorney and historian, to secure the names of the participants in the Battle of Velasco. In fact, none of the work could have been accomplished without the interest and help of his widow, Mrs. Josephine W. Wilson, who not only made available Mr. Wilson's voluminous notes but through the years has given me many of his rare books.

Mrs. Adele Caldwell, a local historian and constant advocate of the preservation of Brazoria County historical treasures, has been helpful not only in advice but in furnishing various manuscripts that would have been impossible to obtain otherwise.

I also had an opportunity to talk with Mrs. Sarah Groce Berlet (a cousin of mine), Abner J. Strobel, and Clarence R. Wharton, all of whom have written histories of the Wharton family. The editor's grandfather, J. P. Bryan, was appointed by Mrs. Sarah Ann Wharton as one of the executors of her will. These persons have given the editor a valuable picture of the Wharton-Groce family history. Twice, the editor had an opportunity to participate in lawsuits which involved the establishment of the Groce heirship.

A great deal of information was made available by the Brazoria County Abstract Company, particularly through the efforts of Mr. and Mrs. D. E. Shepherd. Mr. Shepherd prepared the information shown on the map of Brazoria County, page 72.

I would also like to acknowledge my indebtedness to Walter K. Hanak for information regarding the early cartography of Texas.

The Dow Chemical Company several years ago supported a project involving research on the early plantation era of Brazoria County, and we have included some of the resultant sketches made by Don Hutson of Lake Jackson, Texas. Mr. and Mrs. William W. Boddie did a great deal of this research and have given me invaluable information. Some of the sketches reproduced here belong to Mrs. Frank T. Smith of Angleton, Texas, and Mrs. G. F. Treadway of Houston.

Mrs. Ulmer, of the Houston Public Library, was helpful in obtaining information regarding the early sketches of Houston.   ,

I would like to thank Mrs. Katherine L. Dall, wife of Curtis B. Dall, from whom the University of Texas acquired the diary, for furnishing me the genealogy of the Dall family.

And last I want to acknowledge my indebtedness to the indispensable reference book the *Handbook of Texas,* compiled by Walter Prescott Webb and H. Bailey Carroll (Austin: The Texas State Historical Association, 1952) for constant reference and invaluable information.

J. P. BRYAN

When was the beautiful, so good;
   And when the moral, so sublime—
When knowledge so diffused abroad
   As now, in all the olden time?

True, there are croakers—some who say
That good at best is only evil;
That be our virtues what they may,
   We are but children of the d***l.

Dishonoring him who made the whole,
   And who sustains it every hour,
Of the vast universe, the soul:
   The good—the great self moving power.

Our story assumes a graver tone,
   And lacks, perchance, poetic fire,
Reflection bears the spirit on;
   'Tis *Genius* only can inspire.

For who that thinks, but soars aloft
   Above this speck of Earth and Time,
And who that *feels,* but wishes oft,
   To taste a life yet more sublime?

PLANTATIONS
IN
BRAZORIA COUNTY

Plantations In Brazoria County

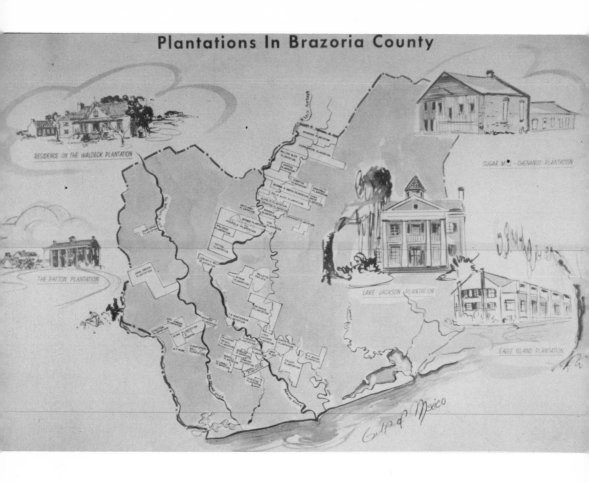

Map showing the location of the principal plantations in Brazoria County.

WALDECK PLANTATION
1871

The Plantation was developed by Morgan L. Smith and later sold by him to Prince Waldeck, a cousin of Queen Victoria.

Patton Plantation. Home of Columbus R. Patton. See Note #10.

Eagle Island Plantation. Home of William H. Wharton. See notes on Sketches #15 and 16.

Lake Jackson Plantation. Home of Abner Jackson. The town of Lake Jackson is now located on the plantation site.

Waldeck Plantation and Sugar Mill. The largest and most modern sugar mill built in Texas during the post-Civil War period.

Ellersly Plantation. Home of J. Greenville McNeel. See Note #162.